BRIDAL STYLE

Text by Nancy Davis

Photo Research by Kathy Farrell-Kingsley

HUGH LAUTER LEVIN ASSOCIATES, INC.

Distributed by Macmillan Publishing Company, New York

Designer: Kathleen Herlihy-Paoli

Picture editor: Leslie Conron Carola

Photo researcher: Kathleen Farrell Kingsley

Production editor: Deborah Zindell

Printed in Hong Kong

ISBN: 0-88363-477-5

ACKNOWLEDGMENTS
~

*A*long the way, dozens of good people helped this book reach the presses by making important contributions — I wish I could name them all. However, a very talented team was required to assemble such a comprehensive overview of weddings: Hugh L. Levin, publisher, who never doubted that all the pieces would fall into place; Leslie Carola, editor, who guided each page and made invaluable decisions; Kathy Kingsley, who compiled the vast array of wonderful photographs; and Kathy Herlihy-Paoli, who gave this book its lovely design.

I must also extend deep thanks to several members of the staff of *Modern Bride* magazine: Cele G. Lalli, editor-in-chief; Mary Ann Cavlin, managing editor; and Debbra Gill, art director. Thanks also to Pamela Nelson of the Museum of the Balch Institute; Laurie Klein; Ilona Toth; Barbara Trafficanda; Mr. and Mrs. Albert W. Davis; and to my husband, Frederick Roffman, and our son, Luke, for their love and support through all those weekends I spent with my computer instead of them.

Photo: Stephane Colbert

~ Contents ~

INTRODUCTION

A wedding is a special celebration that serves as a window to your individual style. The way you choose to celebrate can reveal your interests, beliefs, attitudes, and hopes. For some brides and grooms, a wedding is a solemn ritual or a tender, private moment; for most, however, it is a meaningful and memorable day filled with joyous commotion.

(Preceding spread) A touch of romance and a hint of fantasy as this couple arrives for their ceremony in a carriage led by a team of white horses. Photo: Georgia Sheron.

(Left) Moments after the ceremony, a bride is embraced wistfully by her father. Photo: Jonathan Farrer;

(Opposite) Perhaps the most honored of traditions: a heartfelt toast to the bride and groom. Photo: Nancy Muller, Rocky Mountain Images.

*Y*our wedding is a distinctive special event that you and your fiancé—through the countless choices you make about the ceremony, the reception, fashions, food, flowers, and music—can make uniquely your own.

*N*aturally, the ceremony itself is the most important part of the event, although frequently it is the briefest. Wedding planning tends to focus on the various celebrations surrounding the service—rehearsal dinners, receptions, or even breakfasts the morning after the wedding. They require the most planning—*and* are the scenes of the most revelry. It may be hard to believe how busy you will be with the seemingly endless decisions, meetings, and phone calls to arrange the details of your wedding. Will it take place in a church or a home or a garden? Will it be during the day or in the evening? Will you have a religious ceremony? Who will participate with you? How many guests will attend? Will you wear an antique ballgown or a modern sheath, a veil or hat or crown of flowers? Will you carry an all-white cascade of roses and lilies or a colorful nosegay of freshly picked favorites? Will your cake be chocolate or lemon or carrot? Will you dance to jazz or rock or country?

*T*he key to all your wedding planning is organization: do a bit of reading, looking, comparing, and talk to your groom and family and friends about what is important to you. As the wedding approaches, try to complete each step on your list of preparations with calm and good humor. Remember that even if the minute-to-minute details of your wedding don't follow the course you've painstakingly set, there are very few mishaps that can mar the beauty of your special day.

~ THE RITUALS ~
RELIGIOUS OR SECULAR?

*S*teeped in tradition and sacred to many, "holy matrimony" is a religious event that for many couples demands a religious service.

*I*n the Roman Catholic church, marriage is one of seven sacraments. Because it is viewed as a very serious commitment, couples are generally required to complete premarital counseling in preparation for their life as husband and wife. A traditional Catholic wedding ceremony is frequently celebrated in conjunction with, or as part of, a special Nuptial Mass, although the mass itself is not required. The priest, the bride and groom, two witnesses, and an exchange of vows are the ingredients that are essential to a Catholic wedding ceremony.

In the Jewish tradition, marriage is also considered sacred, and although the ceremony may vary within the religion's Orthodox, Conservative, and Reform groups, the

basic ritual is the same. The bride and groom stand under a *huppah*, or wedding canopy, during the service. Hebrew blessings are recited over wine that is shared by the couple; the bride then receives her wedding ring. The *ketubah*, or marriage contract, is read aloud, followed by the recitation of the Seven Blessings. The ceremony ends with the groom breaking a glass underfoot to symbolize the destruction of the Holy Temple in Jerusalem. This final act, in the happiest of moments, also serves to remind the couple that life can be very fragile.

With the exception of the Episcopal church, Protestant religions do not consider marriage a sacrament. It is, however, viewed as a holy union, with the ceremony based on passages from the Old and New Testaments. The service can be as short as ten minutes, or significantly longer, depending on the liturgy appropriate for certain denominations, or on the choices of the bride and groom. Whatever the duration, the basic ceremony contains three parts: the gathering words and opening prayers; the exchange of vows and rings; and the blessing of the couple and benediction.

Many wedding ceremonies share common rituals, regardless of religious or cultural differences. For instance, the use of wine is widespread. An African-American wedding tradition of pouring a libation to invoke a blessing from the gods parallels the recitation of

(Left) Blessings are bestowed by the priest during a Catholic wedding ceremony. Photo: Maureen DeFries for Laurie Klein Gallery.

(Opposite) At this Jewish service, the groom breaks a glass underfoot to symbolize the destruction of the Holy Temple of Jerusalem. Photo: Christine Newman.

Hebrew blessings over wine at a Jewish service and the offering of wine to God at the Catholic Nuptial Mass or the Episcopalian service.

*A*nother shared theme is the symbolic act of creating a union. Laotian couples are joined at the wrists by a "spiritual string"; a ritual cloth is used to wrap the wrists of the Ukrainian bride and groom; and at conventional Hindu weddings, the couple's hands are tied with a red thread and placed over a vessel that is filled with water, leaves, fruits, and flowers—what are considered to be the essentials of life. The fact that such traditions are still recognized today attests to the endurance of marriage as a social institution, rich in meaning.

*A*ll religions, from Judaism to Islam, Hinduism to Buddhism, and all the many divisions of Christianity—Roman Catholic, Eastern Orthodox, Baptist, Mormon, Methodist, Seventh Day Adventist, or Quaker, among many others—extol marriage as a joyous celebration. Ceremonies vary greatly in their content and symbolic gestures, but similar feelings—those of unity and devotion—will be present at any religious service you plan.

*N*ot everyone, however, wants a storybook wedding, complete with a multitude of bridesmaids and elaborate preparations. If you are one of these couples, a civil ceremony is the chosen route. The reasons may range from personal choice to religious differences, but a civil service can be certainly no less memorable or important or lacking in celebration.

*A*mong the authorized officials who may perform civil ceremonies are judges, justices of the peace, county clerks, and mayors. Although a judge is likely to hold the service in his or her chambers, the ceremony could take place at almost any location you wish, providing the official is willing. The marriage license bureau in your area will provide you with a list of available officials.

~ TRADITIONS AND CUSTOMS ~

To some people, the familiar traditions and customs are simply silly superstitions. Others hold them as powerful rituals to be closely followed in order to assure a happy union. Whatever personal significance they may hold, wedding traditions have obscure, sometimes mystical histories that only add to their popularity.

Many of today's traditions originated in ancient Greece and Rome. They are highly symbolic and largely deal with fertility, sexuality, and good old-fashioned magic.

The custom of the bride wearing "something old, something new, something borrowed, something blue," for example, is taken from an old English rhyme. Interpretations may vary, but, generally, "old" and "borrowed" are thought to honor past traditions; a "new" item will hopefully bring luck in the future; and "blue" has been a symbol of fidelity and modesty, as it was in ancient Israel where it was customary for brides to trim their wedding robes with blue ribbons.

Food has its place among the honored traditions as well. Rice, a symbol of fertility, has been quite often thrown at the couple as they leave their ceremony, although, now, more environmentally conscious wedding guests toss birdseed or rose petals. The gesture of

(Opposite) In a beautiful summer setting, these newlyweds are seen leaving their waterside wedding site. Photo: Stephane Colbert.

(Right) Overgrown with pretty foliage, countryside ruins made a romantic spot for this wedding. Photo: Laurie Klein.

throwing something on the bride and groom is a metaphor for showering them with the good things of life. In Asia, the use of rice signifies a "full pantry." Following Italian and Greek customs, the almond, once a symbol of undying love and youth, is still sugarcoated and given as reception favors to wedding guests.

The lore surrounding some wedding traditions is not entirely romantic. For instance, engagement rings originally indicated that the groom-to-be had basically purchased his fiancée; the woman was seen to be his exclusive property by virtue of wearing his ring. And, once the wedding ceremony took place, the same ring served as the wedding band. It was in the eighth century that the first recorded giving of the engagement "ring" was discovered in the Jewish tradition: a groom gave his bride-to-be a coin to show that he was financially secure.

Not surprisingly it was the French who first associated the ring with love. In sixteenth- and seventeenth-century Europe, gimmal rings were popular signs of engagement. This type of ring with joined or interlocked parts could be divided in two—one half worn by the woman, the other half by the man. Later, the separate rings could be joined and worn together by the woman as her wedding ring.

The diamond engagement ring often associated with today's betrothals did not fully come into fashion until the mid-nineteenth century, when the South African diamond mines opened. Before that, diamonds had been far too scarce and expensive. The year 1477, however, marks the first time a woman was the lucky recipient of an engagement ring with a precious jewel as part of its design. As the famous story goes, Archduke Maximilian of Austria was

(Left) This contemporary wedding party is clearly free of the ancient custom that required attendants to dress like the bride in order to confuse the evil spirits. Photo: Ellis-Taylor Photographers.

(Opposite) The wedding cake has ancient roots and varied symbolism. This creation, by Ellen Baumwoll of Bijoux Doux Specialty Cakes in New York City, shows how these confections have evolved into sweet marvels of art. Photo: The Carlyle Hotel, New York City.

so busy making war that he presented Mary of Burgundy with a diamond ring already in his possession—he simply did not have time to find anything else. Until that time in European society, women had not been permitted to wear rings that contained gems.

The perfectly circular shape of the wedding band itself has long been the symbol of endless love. Early records note that the rings worn by the ancient Egyptians were made of iron, steel, brass, copper, silver, and gold, as well as of less durable materials such as leather and rush. Then, the band was placed on the third finger of the left hand, as it is today. The ancients believed that one vein ran from that finger straight to the heart.

Surprisingly, evil spirits have played a major role in the development of many wedding traditions. In the days of ancient Rome, unseen tricksters were thought to lurk about, posing a threat to the bride and groom. The current practice of inviting men and women to be members of the wedding party evolved from one old Roman custom that required that ten witnesses be present at a marriage ceremony in order to outsmart jealous demons. The bride's attendants dressed in clothes similar to her own, and the same was true of the groom and his ushers. It was hoped that the spirits waiting to rob the couple of their

(Left) Entrusted with a most serious responsibility, this ring bearer leads the wedding processional. Photo: Maureen DeFries for Laurie Klein Gallery.

(Opposite) A glowing bride poses for a wedding portrait, flanked by her attendants and flower girl. Photo: Michael Kohl.

happiness would be confused by the similar clothing and not be able to carry out their wicked plans. To thwart the spirits further, the Romans performed the chivalrous act of carrying the bride safely across the threshold to prevent the jealous spirits from tripping her and spoiling her joy.

The earliest grooms practiced marriage by capture. A bride was "stolen" and taken into hiding until family and friends called off their search for her. The term *honeymoon* has its origins in the period that followed the "capture." For thirty days (or one full moon), the newlyweds drank mead, a brew made by the ancient Gauls and Anglo-Saxons from fermented honey and water. Mead, which is still used in Ireland to toast newlyweds as they depart for their honeymoon, was said to have powers of virility and fertility.

The custom of having a "best man" is believed to date back to wedding captures as well. A friend of the groom was needed to fight off and stall the bride's family while the couple made an escape.

The garter toss, another wedding custom, has its roots in an old British ritual called "flinging the stocking." After the wedding, guests would storm the bridal chamber and snatch the couple's stockings, which the guests then took turns flinging at the newlyweds' faces. The first stocking to touch the bride's or groom's nose would belong to the next to marry. Today, the bride's bouquet toss carries on that custom: it is thought that the single woman who catches the bouquet will marry soon.

Tying cans and shoes to the newlyweds' car remains a popular prank carried out by friends and family. The noise of these items dragging along is meant to chase away evil spirits. In an early Anglo-Saxon ritual, the bride presented the groom with one of her slippers, which he then hung over their bed. This act symbolized the transfer of responsibility for the bride from her father to her new husband.

~ ETHNIC AND ~ CULTURAL INFLUENCES

*T*he impact that families and forebears still have on American weddings is proof of strong emotional ties to individual heritages. Ethnic practices, religious or social, are continually woven into ceremonies by new generations who choose to honor the old.

A comprehensive study of weddings rich in cultural history was cosponsored by The Balch Institute for Ethnic Studies in Philadelphia, and *Modern Bride* magazine. Titled "Something Old, Something New: Ethnic Weddings in America," the 1987 exhibition covered a wide variety of nationalities in marvelous detail. In the show's catalog, Pamela Nelson of the Museum of the Balch Institute notes: "For many immigrant groups, weddings are an occasion at which ethnic traditions can be affirmed and communally celebrated. Yet most groups have acceded to certain changes wrought by their new American values and lifestyles. Whether the bride wears a white wedding gown and marches down the aisle to 'Here Comes the Bride,' or whether she remains faithful to her traditional ethnic customs which, however, no longer hold the same real-life significance for her, Americanization has meant change."

The myriad of interesting ethnic customs still observed lend great insight into the diverse practices of foreign lands. Many are joyful, some seem sad, but all are important threads that reveal a rich tapestry of tradition. The Balch Institute's exhibition recorded many such customs being honored in America today. For example:

- In the Pakistani culture, where arranged marriages were the norm, Muslim custom dictates that the bride and groom, who have never previously met, view each other for the first time in a mirror. Modern Pakistanis who marry for love may still carry out this ritual.
- Lithuanians traditionally hang the matchmaker in effigy, and today, although no such facilitator may have been involved in the courtship, the custom is often ceremoniously staged.
- The traditional Chinese ceremony of obligation requires the bride and groom to bow to heaven and earth and their ancestors, then to their grandparents and parents. The couple serves tea to each relative and receives jewelry and "lucky money" in return.
- At Ukrainian wedding receptions, a traditional ritual involves "kidnapping" the bride and then returning her for ransom. After the wedding, the couple's parents offer them bread and salt, symbols of life's sustenance.
- At both Greek and Thai weddings, the newlyweds wear crowns that are linked together by a ribbon or string.
- The Japanese Shinto wedding rite revolves around the ceremonial exchange of *sake* nine times.
- Just after the Korean wedding ceremony, the bride's mother-in-law gives her red dates to eat, a symbol of fertility.
- At the preliminary ceremony before a Cambodian wedding (many of which are still arranged), the bride endures a symbolic haircutting meant to drive away evil spirits.
- Before a traditional Albanian marriage, the bride's youngest brother places a shoe on her foot, and a representative of the groom slips a ring on her finger. This is a solemn moment, since the bride's family does not attend the wedding or reception—they return home after surrendering her.
- At Lubavitcher Hasidic weddings, a divider separates the men and women at the reception, with joyful merrymaking on both sides as guests dance and wave. The bride and groom

are lifted by guests on tables or chairs so they may see each other over the divider.

☙ *A* chanting priest leads a Greek couple three times around in a circle, representing eternity; they are considered married after the third go-round.

☙ *A*t the end of the wedding reception for many couples of Eastern European heritage, the bride's veil is removed and replaced by a kerchief, signifying that she is now a married woman. This gesture was once marked by sadness, but now is done for the fun of observing tradition.

☙ *M*any African-Americans still "jump the broom" at wedding ceremonies, a custom that originated in the South during the Civil War. The broom is placed on the floor and the couple jumps over it into a state of matrimony.

☙ *A*ll the guests stand during a Russian Orthodox wedding since there are no pews in the sect's traditional churches. The first part of the service is a religious ceremony that pronounces the bride and groom formally engaged. Later, ushers hold bejeweled crowns over the couple's heads.

☙ *A* Hispanic groom may give thirteen coins to his bride—one for Christ and each of his twelve disciples—to show that he will support her.

*T*he wonderful wedding rituals that mark the world's many different religions and cultures compose a long and fascinating list. Thankfully, these rituals have endured, and wisely, new generations continue to embrace them, making America richer still.

☙ *(Opposite) A table for two: Just married, this bride and groom's conversation turns to kisses. Photos: Laurie Klein.*

☙ *(Right) Their play interrupted with a peak out the window, these little girls witness a romantic moment between bride and groom. Photo: Maureen DeFries for Laurie Klein Gallery.*

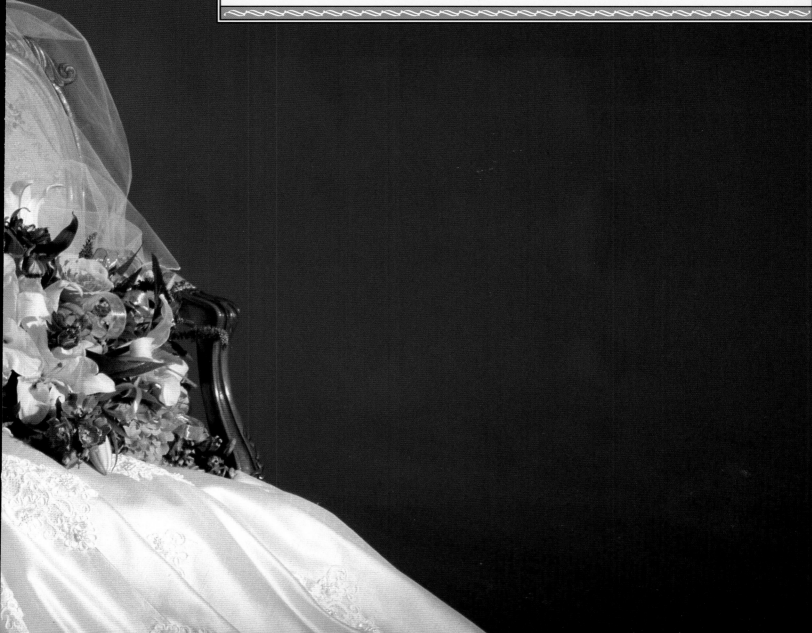

WEDDING FASHIONS

From the moment you first appear at your wedding ceremony until your last wave good-bye, the lines of your gown, the silhouette of your veil, and the lustre of your jewelry reflect all the beauty and romance of the occasion. Assembling such an important ensemble in just the style you envision can be a wonderfully exciting prospect.

❧ (Preceding spread) On- or off-the-shoulder pouf sleeves edge the sweetheart neckline on this ivory silk shantung dress. Designer: Jim Hjelm/A Private Collection.

❧ (Left) Pearl-tipped leaves encircle the shoulders of a handwoven ivory silk gown from the Signature Collection by Rani for St. Pucchi. Photo: Iraida Icaza.

~ THE WEDDING GOWN ~

*O*f all the elements that serve to create a memorable wedding, none may be as important to you as your bridal gown. The object of everyone's gaze and the focus of most of the photographs, it is the one item that can make you look as radiant as you feel—even if you choose to wear a suit, a simple dress, or an outfit of sentimental value.

A LOOK TO THE PAST

*A*lthough for the most part design details remain consistent, bridal silhouettes do change with the times, and wedding attire has gone through many transformations in style and color. General fashion styles of the period, mores, and personal taste have all influenced the wedding gown at different stages in history.

*I*n medieval times, brides often wore the brightly colored fashionable robes of the day. Today's traditional white wedding dress first appeared in the 1820s, although other colors remained popular as well. For those who chose to wear the new whites, advice was widely available. In 1894, *The Ladies Home Journal* suggested: "When wearing a white gown thought must be given to the becomingness of the shade, for, after all, there are as many tints in white as in other colors; the one that may suit the pale blonde is absolutely unbecoming to the rosy brunette.

"*D*ead white, which has a glint of blue about it, is seldom becoming to anyone. It brings out the imperfections of the complexion, tends to deaden the gloss of the hair, and dulls the brightness of the eyes. The white that touches on the cream or coffee shade is undoubtedly the most artistic and best suited to the general woman."

*E*xhibits of wedding gowns past and present are occasionally presented at museums

Before the 1940s and the advent of new designs in bridal attire, the styles of bridal gowns generally followed the fashions of the times. This 1929 bride carried the flapper look through to her wedding dress. Photo: Division of Costume, Smithsonian Institution.

and might serve to give you a helpful overview. As curator of the Stamford Historical Society in Connecticut, Karen Donnelly organized one such show in 1992 called "Wedding Belles: Bridal Fashions Then and Now." That sampling of gowns highlighted many aspects of fashions of the past. "White dresses came into popularity when Queen Victoria married in 1840," says Donnelly. "Although white had always been a choice, many other colors were worn at that time as well. Brides simply wore their best dresses, regardless of the color."

Godey's Lady's Book, the fashion magazine of the Victorian period, also set color trends. For instance, brides who read *Godey's* around 1886 would have found that blues and browns were popular color choices for their gowns.

A bride from 1876 is surrounded by fabric, veiling, and finery. Photo: Division of Costume, Smithsonian Institution.

As for the style of wedding dresses, contemporary fashion generally dictated the design. And, since so many dresses were made by hand, styles changed much more slowly than they do today. "Wedding gowns echoed the stylistic trend of day fashions," adds Donnelly. "Hoops in day dresses became popular after the Civil War, and this was reflected in wedding gowns. Billowy leg-of-mutton sleeves were in vogue at the close of the century in day styles, so they were seen in wedding dresses as well. This pattern remained until roughly the 1940s. After that, a divergent trend was seen: where calf-length dresses may have been the style of the day, long dresses were still worn at weddings."

At the start of the nineteenth century, lighter fabrics were used to accommodate new styles. "Dresses were less tailored and fit loosely, so materials which hung softly suited their design," says Polly Willman, senior conservator of costumes at The National Museum of American History at the Smithsonian Institution in Washington, D.C.

A look at White House brides through the 1800s reveals this trend towards lighter, more flowing gowns. "When Sarah York Jackson married the adopted son of Andrew Jackson in Philadelphia in 1831, she wore a skirt of silk chiffon embroidered with a

Beauty can be seen in the simplest details: this satin gown has scalloped edges on a fitted bodice that leads to a deep V-back. A row of pretty bows lines the skirt and its sweeping train. Designer: Michele Vincent Inc.

silk floss thread," notes Willman. "Decorative bands of grape motifs and wheat sheaths—very characteristic of that period—trimmed the design. In the mid 1860s, President Buchanan's niece, Harriet Lane Johnson, was married in a gown of stunning moiré taffeta. And for the wedding of President Cleveland in 1886, his wife, Frances, wore a gown whose surface was silk-faced satin with a cotton ground. The fabric, called bridal satin, had more weight as a result of the added cotton."

Another favored fabric for early Victorian wedding dresses was silk in all its varieties, often trimmed with lace. Honiton lace, one of several types of this delicate fabric made primarily in the Netherlands, was incorporated into the design of Queen Victoria's famous white gown, making laces another fashionable feature for the rest of the nineteenth century—and beyond.

SHAPING YOUR VISION

Because your gown is likely to be the most elaborate and luxurious article of clothing you ever purchase, you will want to consider all the options available. To help you sort through the possibilities, here are some things to keep in mind as you shop.

To begin, it is best to be a bit cautious about where you buy your wedding gown. Unless you are wearing an heirloom, having your gown custom-made or making it yourself, you'll be visiting one or more bridal retail stores. A reliable, full-service bridal salon will

assist you in every step from discussing current bridal styles to overseeing your own final fitting. You will be paying for quality and expertise—and perhaps peace of mind. Buying from a bargain resource could leave much to chance when purchasing such a supremely important item. Of course, a reliable dressmaker can handle the alterations, if necessary.

It is important to realize that most bridal gowns commonly arrive twelve weeks after they have been ordered. While some manufacturers take longer, others may deliver in eight to ten weeks. In either case, it's wise to keep the twelve-week mark in mind once your date is set.

Since every detail of your wedding gown reflects your personal style, it is best to consider in depth all of the possible variations in color, fabric, silhouette, skirt length, sleeves, and neckline. The following definitions of clothing design terms will give you a clearer understanding of your choices.

White still reigns as the favored color for a gown, with variations of cream and off-white shades ranking next in popularity. Satin, silk, organza, organdy, taffeta, velvet, chiffon, lace, cotton, linen, tulle, and rich brocades are just some of the fabrics that you may touch during the search for your gown. Some dresses simply rely on the beauty of the fabric and the lines of the gown to make a statement. Others may be trimmed with a sprinkling of sequins, beads, pearls, or crystals. Scrolls of embroidered passementerie (a fancy edging or trimming made of braid, cord, beading, or metallic thread), fabric flowers, satin cording, rich ribbons or bows may also be used.

Soft lines, picture perfect: a wedding gown lavished with beaded lace through the bodice and sweeping skirt. Pearl clusters trim soft, pleated sleeves that edge an off-the-shoulder neckline. Designer: Michele Piccione for Alfred Angelo Dream Maker.

The Line

- *Empire silhouette* refers to a dress style with a high waistline that starts just under the bustline and is usually defined by a seam.
- *Princess line* refers to a classic silhouette that is shaped with vertical seams. It fits snugly through the rib cage, has a seamless waist, then flares slightly to the hem.
- A *sheath* is a straight, body-hugging gown, often floor-length; it is sometimes designed with a train that may or may not detach.
- A *strapless gown* is designed to bare the shoulders. This elegant style is often topped with a coordinating jacket.

The Skirt

- A *bouffant skirt* is a very full skirt, gathered at the waist, and usually worn over a crinoline.

❧ A *ballgown skirt* is a style designed with a natural waistline and a very full, flared skirt.

❧ An *intermission-length skirt*, which is also called a hi-lo skirt, falls midcalf in front, then extends to the floor in back.

❧ A *tiered skirt* has a series of layers or flounces that fall in graduated rows.

The Train

❧ A *bustle* is a skirt with a gathering of fabric, ruffles, or other design details that fill out the back.

❧ A *train* is formed by fabric that is either part of the skirt or detachable and that trails in back of the gown.

❧ A *sweep train* is a short train that "sweeps" the floor.

❧ A *chapel train* is one that extends one and a third yards from the waist.

❧ A *cathedral train* is one that extends three yards from the waist.

The Sleeve

❧ A *cap sleeve* is a short, fitted sleeve that just barely covers the shoulders.

❧ A *cape sleeve* is a sleeve achieved by placing a circular piece of fabric over each shoulder and then stitching it to the bodice, giving a caped effect over each arm.

❧ *Poufed sleeves* can be long or short, very full at the top.

❧ A *fitted-point sleeve* is a long sleeve that falls just below the wrist, descending to a point.

❧ A *Juliet sleeve* is a long sleeve poufed at the shoulder but fitted on the forearm.

❧ A *petal sleeve* is a short sleeve made of overlapping panels that are curved at the hem, creating a petal-shaped effect.

The Waistline

❧ A *natural waistline* is a waist with a seam at the narrowest part of the midriff—at the point of the natural waistline.

❧ A *basque waistline* is an elongated waist that dips to a V-shaped point at the center of the front of the dress.

❧ A *dropped waistline* is a waist with a slightly gathered seam line several inches below the natural waistline.

The Neckline

❧ An *illusion yoke* has transparent lace or netting fitted at the neckline and shoulders, often extending down to the bustline.

❧ An *on-or off-the-shoulder neckline* is one that can be worn up on the shoulders or down.

❧ A *jewel neckline* is rounded to follow the natural contours of the neck, creating a simple background for jewels.

❧ A *wedding band–collar* is a traditional stand-up band that circles the neck.

❧ A *sabrina neckline* is a straight neckline beginning two inches inside of the shoulder edge.

❧ A *sweetheart neckline* is a moderately low neckline that begins two inches from the shoulder edge and has a heart-shaped center front.

❧ A *portrait collar* is a neckline fabric that frames the shoulders, often gathered in the center above the bustline with a decorative fabric detail or ornament.

❧ A *scoop neck* is a low, curved neckline cut deep in the front, back, or both.

❧ A *U-back* is a plunging, U-shaped scoop design on the back of a gown.

Finding Your Style
*B*ridal designers create gowns to flatter any bride. For this day of days, choose a style that will enhance your features and complement your body type. With such a wide variety of styles available, some general guidelines may be helpful.

🌿 *If* you are short and thin, a gown, perhaps sleeveless, with a high waistline and neckline will make you look taller. If you are short with a few extra pounds, stay away from flounced skirts, and try a high-necked, blouson bodice over a fitted slip with a slightly gathered waist to lengthen your lines.

🌿 *The* billowy, layered look generally looks best on a tall, thin bride, who can carry a bare, off-the-shoulder style and a dramatic dropped waist.

🌿 *A* simple, soft look complements any figure type. The vertical lines of the princess cut with a natural or high neckline are always appropriate. If you want to minimize your weight, avoid too much lace, beading, and puffed sleeves.

🌿 *And* if you are of average height and weight, try them all. The best advice for any bride is: select a gown you really love, and you'll look lovely in it.

～ A HEADPIECE AND VEIL ～

*H*eadpieces, like the gowns they enhance, range from classic to contemporary, with many modifications along the way. The style you ultimately choose should complement your gown, flatter your face, and be comfortable enough to wear from ceremony through reception.

If possible, when you try on headpieces have your hair styled the way you will be wearing it on your wedding day. Matching your hairstyle to the mood and style of the headpiece is an important detail not to be overlooked. While actually experimenting with choices at the shop is the best way to determine the right style, there is one guideline that usually applies: simpler headpieces generally complement more dramatic dresses, while more detailed ones may work well with classic, understated looks.

The basic types of headpieces are all subject to a variety of trims, so that each is highly individual. These variations help ensure that the headpiece you choose will personalize your own wedding attire. In addition to a tiara, which resembles a crown, other choices include a headband, comb, picture hat, pillbox hat, Juliet cap, mantilla, wreath, snood, or fresh flowers.

*V*eils are designed in a variety of lengths and can be secured to your headpiece. The more elaborate veils are often made to be detachable so they can be removed for the reception—an important consideration in light of a bride's wish to dance and socialize. The

🌿 *(Opposite) A U-shaped back, a row of pearl buttons, and scrolled lace that accentuate a graceful neck are some of the masterful touches that compose this beautiful bridal image. Designer: Michele Piccione for Alfred Angelo Dream Maker.*

*Bridal
Style*

❧ *The headpiece should complement the gown and suit the bride's hairstyle. This headband of lace and beads carries a pouf crown of illusion—the same elements seen in the wedding dress. Photo: Chicago Bead Works.*

following lengths are among the most frequently chosen: *birdcage* (ends just below the chin); *flyaway* (brushes the shoulders); *fingertip* (brushes the tips of the fingers); and *ballet* or *waltz* (extends to the knee). A *blusher* is the delicate veil worn over the bride's face that is lifted during the ceremony. And for the most formal gowns, veils that trail behind the bride are also available in several lengths.

～ FASHION ACCESSORIES ～

On your wedding day, adornment can seem an art with accessories that are packed with panache. Naturally, the selection of your gown comes first, but the shoes, gloves, purse, and jewelry you wear with it can be every bit as important. They add the finishing touches to complete the look you desire.

SHOES

Ask any bride who has stood, danced, and greeted her way through her wedding day what you should know about shoes and her first word is sure to be *comfort*. Try not to make a drastic change from the heel height you're accustomed to. If you can generally be found in flats, chances are that a high heel may spoil some of your fun. Should you decide to wear a different heel, make sure the shoe fits well in every way.

Your choice of footwear also needs to be practical depending on the type of reception you have planned. For instance, if you are having an outdoor ceremony or reception, you would find it difficult to walk on grass wearing heels. It is also wise to buy your shoes soon after you've bought a gown: that way, you'll have plenty of time to break them in around the house, and it will also be helpful to wear them at scheduled dress fittings.

Wedding shoes are one purchase that many brides are able to use again. At the Peter Fox bridal shoe store in New York City, for example, wedding styles are based on Fox's everyday collection, and all shoes are made in dyeable fabrics. Transforming bridal shoes into basic black for future evening events is a favorite choice, as well as a money saver.

Embedded with beadwork from heel to toe, these pearly pumps are traced with gold details. Shoes: Dyeables. Photo: Marili Forastieri.

For your wedding day itself, however, your shoes—made of satin, brocade, or silk—may display details such as soutache (a narrow braid with a herringbone pattern), ribbons, bows, braids, beads, and jeweled ornaments. Linda Sarro, manager of Fox's shop, notes that each year the preferred types of trim and decoration change. "Last year, brides loved sequined shoes; this year, simple bows are favored. But as for heel heights, the two-and-a-quarter-inch medium heel remains our most popular. It gives you a bit of lift and makes you feel more elegant than flats. It also works with a variety of dress lengths."

HANDBAGS

Once the celebrating begins, there are only a few necessities the bride may need to reach for. A brush, lipstick, handkerchief, or even medication, can be carried along in style in a beautiful handbag.

Today's designers have made it easy to find just the right bag, from an opulent little purse to a charming shape done in rich fabric. Carey Adina, a New York City designer known for the whimsical silhouettes in her everyday collection (flower pots, top hats, and pyramids, among others), has translated many of them into bridal colors and brocades that will accent any wedding. "The bride's bag adds a finishing grace note. And the most stunning new shapes are both functional as well as fashionable, with chain straps *and* wrist straps so they don't get in the way at receptions."

Handbag fabrics include silk, linen, satin, leather, straw, and lace. The one you choose will depend on the formality of your wedding, the style of your gown and, of course, your personal preference. Adina likes "gold or silver kid because a bride can use it again as a wonderful evening bag. But, I think the most sophisticated of all choices is the *minaudière* clutch. It has a drop-in chain and looks perfectly elegant when placed on the table. However, that's not to say that a bride's accessories must necessarily be demure. They can make whatever fashion statement you choose, from ladylike to outrageous. There's no point in planning this big day and not expressing your personality!"

• Like an intricate mosaic, this beaded bridal handbag incorporates a touch of soft color through a floral motif. Photo: Georgia Sheron.

GLOVES

For many women, gloves were once an indispensible accessory. During the 1930s and 1940s, no outfit was complete, day or night, without a pair in cotton, kid, satin, or lace. Today, gloves are generally reserved for only the most formal of occasions, such as weddings.

The etiquette of gloves was once dictated by the formality of the wedding, time of the ceremony, and style of the gown. Today, your gown's sleeve length seems to be the only determining factor. "I've found that brides still take gloves very seriously," says La Crasia, owner of La Crasia Gloves, Inc., the last bridal glove manufacturer still operating in this country. "They were part of dress-up as a little girl, and today they're still important for a pulled-together look."

Although gloves come in a wide variety of colors, fabrics, and lengths, La Crasia reports that her most popular model is consistently a basic stretch, matte, opera-length glove in white or ivory. Since this glove extends to the armpit, it can only be worn with a strapless or cap-sleeved gown. Other favored looks are shirred satin elbow-length gloves and a shorter style that extends four inches from the wrist, ending in an organza ruffle. For long-sleeved gowns, a short net glove is often the preferred choice among her customers.

When you pose for photographs or walk down the aisle, gloves can lend a graceful accent, but you may be concerned about what to do once you reach the altar. La Crasia explains: "The gloves must be removed during the ceremony for the wedding ring, unless the bride has chosen a very fine crochet over which the ring can be placed. But we've designed kidskin gloves with the stitching removed from the ring finger; the leather is then folded into the glove during the exchange of rings and later stitched back on at our showroom."

This bride's new elbow-length gloves complete the well-known picture: in her hands — something old, something borrowed, and something blue. Photo: Georgia Sheron.

JEWELS

There's something about a beautiful dress, suit, or gown that calls for elegant adornment — and jewels generally top the list of options.

The jewelry you wear on your wedding day may be decided by the formality of your ceremony and reception, the lines of your gown, or even the style of your hair. You may already own some lovely pieces or receive a wedding-day gift from your groom or be given an heirloom with special meaning.

Whatever your personal choices, Claire Kellam, executive vice president of Christian Dior Jewelry, recommends that brides follow these guidelines when making their decisions:

- If your dress has an elaborately detailed bodice, you may want to forego a necklace and focus instead on earrings. The more detailed the dress, the simpler the earrings, and vice versa.
- When choosing earrings, keep stature and scale in mind. If you are petite, choose more delicate looks, such as drop pearls. Taller women can carry bigger styles, such as a large, single pearl or a dramatic pearl cluster.
- A simple bodice often calls for a necklace. Certainly, a strapless or off-the-shoulder gown requires something around the neck—perhaps a double-strand pearl choker.
- If your dress is strapless or has short sleeves, you may want to wear a bracelet. Consider a single- or double-strand pearl design.
- Where your bridesmaids are concerned, a gift of jewelry can accomplish several things: it may serve as a beautiful memento and also lend a uniform look to the wedding party—if that's something you desire.

Pearls

Pearls are the lustrous gems that most often come to mind when it's time to choose wedding day jewels. Whether a simple strand for a portrait collar, or earrings set with rhinestones, pearls often make the perfect statement. They are both romantic and traditional and, since ancient times, have been treasured as symbols of purity and modesty. Here, as with most other bridal accessories, there are several categories to consider.

Natural pearls are formed when an irritant, such as a grain of sand, finds its way into an oyster shell. Tissue lining the shell secretes a substance known as nacre to coat the object and reduce the irritation. Many layers and several years later, an extremely rare pearl is completed. *Cultured* pearls are created by the same natural process; however, the irritant is deliberately introduced. *Simulated* pearls are manufactured through a variety of procedures that determine their quality and price.

Although pearls are incorporated into many pieces of jewelry, the most common choice for a bride is the necklace. If you intend on purchasing one just for this occasion, first consider various lengths that will work with the style of the neckline and bodice of your

dress. Popular lengths are: the *collar* (multiple strands that fit closely around the neck); the *choker* (14 to 15 inches long); *princess* (18 inches long); *matinee* (22 to 23 inches long); *opera* (30 to 36 inches long); and *rope* (any necklace longer than opera-length).

Whether pearls, diamonds, rubies, or sapphires, the wedding jewels you choose will add flair to your attire that day and remain forever as special keepsakes.

This single, princess-length strand of pearls is a classic jewelry choice for an off-the-shoulder wedding gown. Dress designer: Michele Piccione for Alfred Angelo Dream Maker.

❧ (Above, left) Dwight and Mamie Eisenhower in their 1916 wedding portrait taken three days after the ceremony. Her simple dress with scalloped tiers and embroidered vest, although not the dress she wore on her wedding day, looks lovely next to the groom's handsome dress whites. Photo: Courtesy of the Dwight D. Eisenhower Library.

❧ (Above, center) A portrait of Mrs. Grover Cleveland in her wedding gown. Photo: C. M. Bell, 1886, Library of Congress.

❧ (Above, right) When President Wilson's daughter Nellie married in 1914, she wore ivory satin trimmed with old lace. Photo: Library of Congress.

❧ (Opposite, left) President Theodore Roosevelt stood by his daughter Alice and her new husband, Nicholas Longworth, for this wedding picture. Photo: E. S. Curtis, Feb. 21, 1906, Library of Congress.

❧ (Opposite, right) This 1942 wedding gown is a column of satin that pools into a shimmering circle at the bride's feet. Photo: Division of Costume, Smithsonian Institution.

🌿 (Below) Tricia Nixon was married to Edward Cox at the White House in 1971. Her straight gown featured a sheer overskirt embroidered with lace motifs. Photo: National Archives/Nixon Library.

🌿 (Top, right) Fashions come full circle: 1960s style—portrait necklines, mid-calf dresses, satin pumps, timeless tuxedos—would be perfectly appropriate at a contemporary wedding. Photo: Division of Costume, Smithsonian Institution.

🌿 (Bottom, right) Short and sweet in 1951: Flower girls in frilly dresses greet the bride, whose sophisticated satin gown is topped with a scalloped, illusion neckline. Photo: Division of Costume, Smithsonian Institution.

🌿 (Opposite) A classic moment captured in time: Jacqueline Bouvier's engagement portrait allows just a glimpse of her stunning gown. Photo: Copyright Bradford Bachrach; The Kennedy Library.

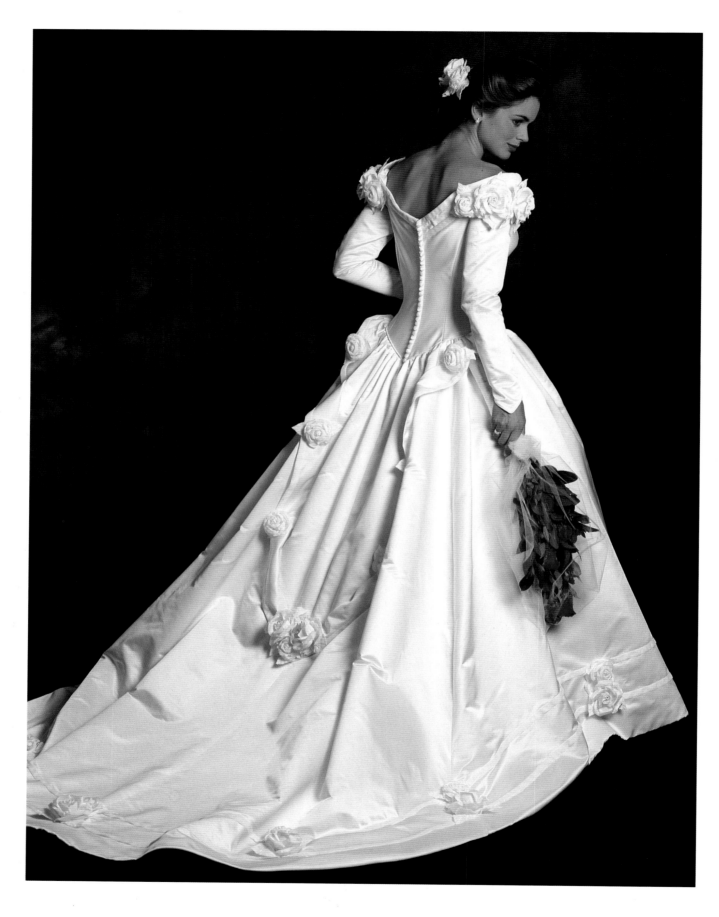

A gown with a beautifully sculpted back makes a lasting impression from the moment the bride enters and throughout the ceremony.

🌺 (Left) Fabric roses are everywhere on this silk satin gown with a tip-of-the-shoulder neckline. Velvet ribbon borders the hem and bodice. Designer: Lora Van Lear Bridals.

🌺 (Opposite) Exquisite attention to detail: A tiered portrait collar circles the shoulders of this blush silk shantung gown. An oversized bow, covered buttons, and silk rosebuds add a touch of genius in back. Designer: Christian Dior Bridal Collection.

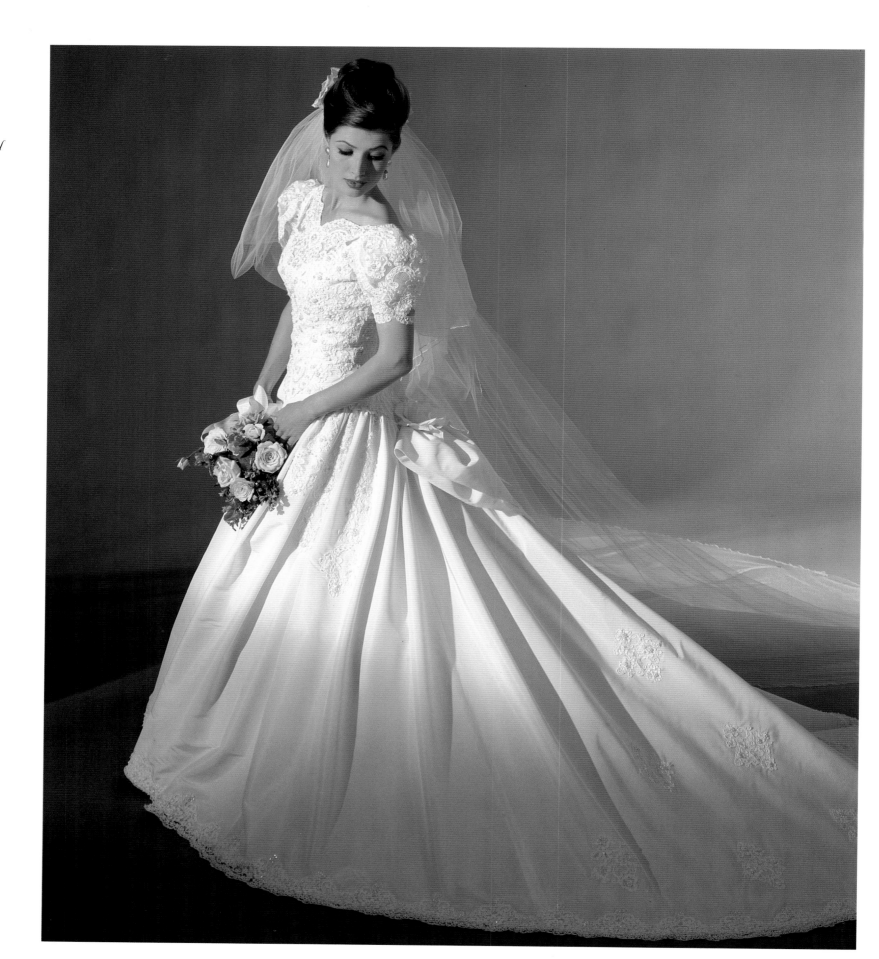

Gowns styled with traditional elements have remained favorites because of their flattering lines.

❧ *(Opposite) A striking gown done in silk peau de soie sparkles with beads and sequins on the bodice and sleeves. Designer: Jim Hjelm/A Private Collection.*

❧ *(Above, left) The natural lines of fine lace form the soft edge of this bride's off-the-shoulder neckline—a perfect complement to the lilacs in her hair. Photo: Marili Forastieri.*

❧ *(Above, right) The full skirt is silk; the decolleté bodice, shaped in lovely Venise lace, just skims the shoulders. Designer: Priscilla of Boston.*

Bridal
Style
~

🎗 (Opposite) The basque waist bodice, with its slenderizing lines, is a classic look. This one is lace dressed up with sequins, and matched with a full skirt. Designer: Lora Van Lear Bridals..

🎗 (Below) In the cummerbund style, this wrapped waist cinches a bodice that's balanced by billowing sleeves. Designer: Dolce & Gabbana.

🎗 (Right, top and bottom) The sweetheart neckline looks beautiful with pendants, chokers, or pearl ropes. Designer: Jim Hjelm/A Private Collection.

Wedding styles on the runway from the couture set reveal a break from tradition—in color, fabric, length, and vision.

❧ *(Top row, from left)* A type of cocoon cape tops a gown by Givenchy Couture; also from Givenchy Couture, a burst of brilliant flowers all wrapped up in a pink waist bow; for springtime brides, Yves St. Laurent's green and white striped gown sashed with a bright green bow; very fitted, very French: the modern bride by Chanel. Photos: Dan Lecca.

❧ *(Bottom row, from left)* A soft green skirt and crisp white blouse by Givenchy Couture. Photo: Dan Lecca. A full train floats behind a bridal short set. Designer: Carolina Herrera. From Lacroix Couture, a flower-trimmed jacket worn with a softly layered gown and wide-brimmed hat. Photo: Dan Lecca; recognizing a Spanish influence this brown, pleated gown is topped with a floor-length lace mantilla. Designer: Carolina Herrera.

❧ *(Opposite)* Pretty in pink: a cloud of tulle shapes the skirt on a gown with a silk satin strapless bodice. The tulle collar can be lifted in back to serve as a hood. Designer: Vera Wang Bridal Collection.

A sheath has form-following lines that cut a slim, sophisticated silhouette. These straight shapes look wonderful with additions such as bustles, overskirts, and trains.

❧ (Opposite, left) Pink tulle borders the neckline and cascades in panels behind the bride in this sleek white style. Photo/designer: Ulla-Maija.

❧ (Opposite, right) This off-the-shoulder column of rich satin has bows down the back and a godet train. Designer: Vera Wang Bridal Collection.

❧ (Below, left) Very contemporary: a fluid crepe sheath with a flared hemline. Sheer, stretch illusion shapes the yoke and sleeves with trumpet cuffs. Photo/designer: Vera Wang Bridal Collection.

❧ (Below, center) This crushed velvet mermaid sheath ends in a flounced satin hem; silk and satin flowers add great dimension. Gown: Robert Legere for The Diamond Collection. Photo: Tim Geaney.

❧ (Below, right) Bow sleeves and a fan-shaped, silk satin cathedral train create a lovely balanced line on this gown of beaded Alençon lace. Designer: Priscilla of Boston.

A suit can be the most fitting choice for a wedding: they're often ideal for less formal affairs, second-time brides, and style setters.

❧ (Above) Proper attire for this western-style wedding in South Carolina meant a pleated white suit for her, a long black coat for him — and, of course, hats and boots to match. Photo: Fridrick Tiedemann.

❧ (Opposite, left) Two pieces compose this softly tailored suit: The skirt features a hi-low hem, the jacket is fashionably styled with peplum. Designer: Michele Vincent Inc.

❧ (Opposite, right) A two-piece pantsuit in fluid rayon crepe shimmers with sequined lapels. Suit: Criscione. Photo: Scott Hagendorf.

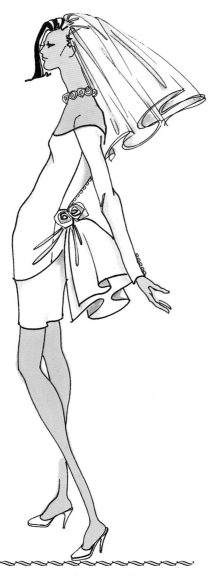

Beautiful examples of how sophisticated short can be.

❧ (Opposite, left) This pink shantung suit may be worn by the bride, her mother, or a guest. Rhinestone buttons and lace-inset sleeves add the necessary glamour. Designer: Michele Piccione for Alfred Angelo Dream Maker.

❧ (Opposite, right) This bride's elegant suit and hat looked just right at her informal afternoon wedding. Photo: Georgia Sheron.

❧ (Above) Off the shoulder and above the knee, this ivory satin tunic dress has a short train in back that's cinched by hand-rolled roses. Designer: Vera Wang Bridal Collection.

❧ (Right) Pearls and sequins sparkle on an all-over lace fitted dress with simple cap sleeves. Designer: Michele Vincent Inc.

For many couples, a departure from the ordinary is the only way to celebrate a wedding.

❧ *(Left)* The groom's chance to turn heads: As part of an otherwise traditional outfit, he chose to wear "formal" shorts and polka dot socks. Photo: Craig Merrill.

❧ *(Above)* For a ceremony in the Caribbean surf, these newlyweds dressed the part: tulle touches for her bathing suit, a boutonniere for his shirt pocket. Photo: Bridget Gallagher for Fantasia Occasions.

❧ *(Opposite)* This couple's favorite spot for photo taking was on a carpet of oyster shells by the bay. Her satin gown has lace insets on the sleeves and around the full skirt. Photo: Fridrick Tiedemann.

The full, pouf sleeve has a very formal look, making it a natural design choice for many bridal dresses.

❧ (Above, left) Roses trim the pleated bodice of a satin gown with a dropped waist, pouf sleeves, and shirred skirt. Gown: Michele Piccione for Alfred Angelo Dream Maker. Photo: Marili Forastieri.

❧ (Above, center) An embroidered white satin wedding gown worn in 1835 features a very full example of the pouf sleeve. Photo: The Metropolitan Museum of Art. Gift of Miss J. H. Rhodes, 1917.

❧ (Above, right) Pouf sleeves, such as those on this beaded gown, are often designed to fit on or off the shoulder. Designer: Michele Vincent Inc.

❧ (Left) Authentic dried roses are tucked into the pouf sleeves and back ruffle of this silk satin gown. Photo/designer: Lora Van Lear Bridals.

❧ (Opposite) This bride's satin and tulle skirt twirls up as she dances with her father. The gown's pouf sleeves are done in delicately embroidered point d'esprit. Photo: Maripat Goodwin Photography.

Wedding fashions through the years.

❧ (Opposite) A regal study in bridal design: This silk brocade shantung gown has an off-the-shoulder bodice of Alençon lace, patterned with sequins and beads. Lace cording traces the neck, sleeves, and waist. Designer: Jim Hjelm/A Private Collection.

❧ (Above) A long train sweeps around this ankle-length gown, c. 1929. Photo: Division of Costume, Smithsonian Institution.

❧ (Right) A more recent interpretation: Hundreds of hand-sewn pearls cover a raw silk bodice with basque waist. The full silk organza skirt has a cuffed hem. Photo/designer: Ulla-Maija.

From locations to dresses, weddings are all about individual style.

❧ (Above, left) Flowers rim the fitted bodice of a taffeta gown topped with a lacy hat. Gown: J. C. Originals. Hat: Erica Koesler. Photo: Marili Forastieri.

❧ (Above, center) A costume with a vintage feeling: a tea-length wedding dress with cutwork embroidery matched with a charming hat. Photo: Georgia Sheron.

❧ (Above, right) A sheer overskirt and sleeves are circled with shimmering satin bands. Designer: Carolina Herrera.

🌢 (Left) Mamie Eisenhower in her wedding gown, complete with picture hat and parasol. Photo: Courtesy of the Dwight D. Eisenhower Library.

🌢 (Above) Captured in this setting, there's a distinctly southern style to an off-the-shoulder gown with tiers of ruffles at the bodice and a sweeping hem. Photo: Joseph C. Pecoraro.

🌢 (Right) A pink cascade of streamers and roses accents the waist of this English net gown. Designer: Christian Dior Bridal Collection.

The image of a long, flowing train trailing behind a glamorous gown often comes to mind when we think of weddings.

❧ (Above) Side draping, beads, and lace adorn a train that is the focus of this off-the-shoulder sheath. Designer: Lili.

❧ (Top, right) A French wedding gown designed by Callot Souers, c. 1930, represents the height of elegance for brides of that period. Photo: The Brooklyn Museum. Gift of Mrs. Russel Davenport.

❧ (Bottom, right) French designer Vionnet combined a wonderful length of silk charmeuse and net for this 1928 gown. Photo: Wadsworth Atheneum, Hartford, Connecticut. Gift of Mr. and Mrs. Burton G. Tremaine.

🐝 *(Below) This type of wrapped shoulder detail, sometimes called a fichu, tops the sheer, lacy yoke of this satin dress by Jessica McClintock. Photo: Tim Geaney.*
🐝 *(Right) Oversized and opulent, this gown's bow with wide streamers accents a dramatic bodice. Designer: Christian Dior Bridal Collection.*

Whether casual country or white tie and tails, each wedding theme reflects a very personal vision.

❧ (Above) The gathered sleeves of this ivory sateen dress—cuffed with lace and trimmed with roses at the shoulders—give it soft appeal. Photo: Courtesy of Laura Ashley.

❧ (Right) A lace overlay tops the bustier bodice of a classically elegant sateen gown. Photo: Courtesy of Laura Ashley.

❧ (Opposite) The layered effect of this lace design, together with the gauntlets, lends this gown a Renaissance feeling. Beaded Alençon and Bristol laces grace the fitted bodice, silk taffeta skirt, and cathedral train. Designer: Priscilla of Boston.

Bridal
Style

Many brides consider the tradition of a veil an essential part of the wedding ceremony.

(Opposite) This ivory veil is encircled with an embroidered floral swag and can be worn at any angle, with more length in front or in back. Here, it floats over a wreath of fresh flowers. Photo: Courtesy of Laura Ashley.

(Above) A headpiece styled of Alençon lace, pearl sprays, and satin is finished with a tulle pouf and a long veil. Photo: Chicago Bead Works.

Simple headpieces and special hats make stylish, contemporary choices.

🌿 *(Above, left) A side comb of roses and beads adds a soft accent. Designer: Michele Piccione for Alfred Angelo Dream Maker.*

🌿 *(Above, center) Pearl-kissed illusion, tucked into a sleek back bun, falls gracefully over the shoulders. Designer: Michele Piccione for Alfred Angelo Dream Maker.*

🌿 *(Above, right) Folds of silk trimmed with tiny pearl clusters create a back comb with understated elegance. Designer: Michele Piccione for Alfred Angelo Dream Maker.*

🌿 *(Opposite) A parade of pink and white roses circle the crown of a poetic broad-brimmed hat by Angie for J&G Bridal Veils. Photo: Bico Stupakoff.*

Gloves, in the wide variety of lengths and fabrics available today, continue to be an important accessory for a "pulled-together look."

❧ (Above) Whether just shy of or full elbow-length, gloves with fanciful details are a great choice to wear with sleeveless or short-sleeved gowns. Here, embroidered ribbons and a tailored pleat create a special look. Gloves: Carolina Amato Accessories. Photo: Mahdavian.

❧ (Opposite, top) Lace is a natural choice of fabric for shaping or trimming any length glove. Another has a flower cuff, and the sheer opera-length style is studded with pearls. Gloves: Carolina Amato Accessories. Photo: Mahdavian.

❧ (Opposite, bottom) A wrapped waist and curved portrait neckline gracefully complement each other on a creamy white gown. Photo: Joseph C. Pecoraro.

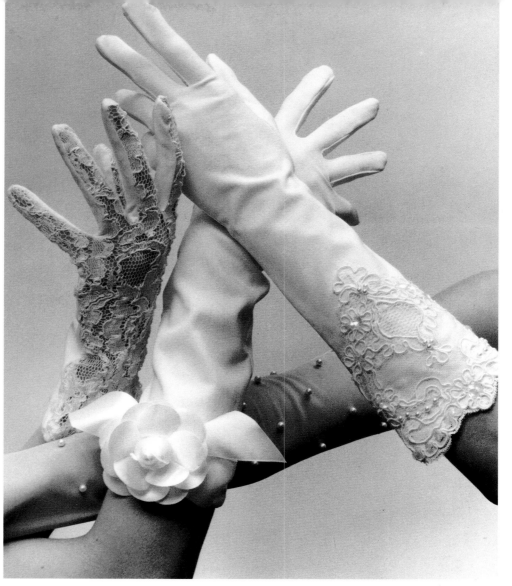

🐝 *(Left) All that glitters, from top: A platinum band with a round diamond in a tension setting by Paul Klecka; a princess-cut diamond flanked by smaller ones, styled by Feature Ring; a gold setting with a pear-shaped diamond and baguettes by M. Grunberg; an emerald-cut diamond and sapphire ring from Tiffany & Co.; a triangular diamond solitaire ring by John Atencio. Photo: Iraida Icaza.*

🐝 *(Above) Wedding bands for a double ring ceremony are tied with satin ribbons: hers has diamonds in a channel setting, his is braided gold. Photo: Maureen DeFries for Laurie Klein Gallery.*

🌿 *(Right) New band leaders, from far left: Diamonds in a pavé setting are divided by delicate bars of gold, by Wright & Lato; white and yellow in a criss-cross mesh design by Krementz & Co.; diamonds set in a band of brushed gold by Whitney Boin; the names of the bride and groom are etched into this gold, platinum, and diamond band from the Love Spell Collection by ArtCarved; a tubular band of platinum and gold by Michael Bondanza. Photo: Iraida Icaza.*

WEDDING RINGS

To some people, the engagement ring is considered the ultimate gift of love. To others, a ring is not even considered a necessary—or desirable—part of "popping the question." Since the majority of brides do receive one, however, it may help for you to know the basics of buying the right gem.

The famous five *C*'s are a good guide for diamond shopping. The first is *cut*, meaning the proportions a rough diamond takes on after being shaped by a skilled expert. Popular cuts include the marquise, oval, round (or brilliant), pear-shaped, and emerald-cut diamonds. Others are the sparkling princess (square), trillion (triangular), and heart-shaped stones. *Carat* weight, or standard measure of a diamond, is 100 points. For example, a 50 point stone is one-half of a carat. The *color* is graded on a scale that ranges from D (colorless "white") to Z (yellow). *Clarity* refers to the absence of natural flaws, such as bubbles, and is evaluated in seven grades, from FL, meaning flawless, to I, imperfect. And *certification* is a diamond grading report that allows you to compare stones before you buy.

Although diamonds have often been set in dazzling designs, other stones are becoming increasingly popular. Emeralds, rubies, sapphires, colored diamonds and birthstones are chosen by many brides and grooms who prefer something unique, less traditional but equally beautiful.

Gold wedding bands are given during the marriage ceremony to seal the union. Once, only the simplest circlets would do. Now, these bands can be found embellished with gems or treated to special finishes such as matte, hammered, or Florentine (textured with a tool).

In addition to design, color must also be considered when selecting bands. Yellow gold is most traditional, but white gold or platinum may be chosen to complement an engagement ring created with the same metal—or simply to stand alone.

In keeping with changing tastes and attitudes, many gold bands now feature one or more diamonds or other precious jewels. These designs serve as both engagement ring and wedding band.

Your wedding jewelry can be traditional or uniquely personal, depending on your preference. Whatever pieces you choose, their lasting beauty and brilliance will be a constant reminder of the commitment you both pledge on this memorable day.

ॐ *(Right) A wedding band is the symbol of lasting love, and there are as many ways to capture that sentiment as there are imaginative designers to give it shape. Top row: Susan Ross Reinstein/Ross, Ltd.; Jane Bohan; Susan Reinstein for Reinstein/Ross, Ltd. Second row: ArtCarved; Hidalgo; Joan Michlin Collection. Third row: Jane Bohan; Mish; Lisa Taubes; Fourth row: Wedding Rings & Company; Mish; Lisa Taubes; Fifth row: Lazaro; ArtCarved; Hidalgo; ArtCarved. Photo: Cynthia Brown.*

Careful consideration is given to wedding-day accessories, particularly jewels and handbags.

🍂 (Opposite, left) A weighty pearl necklace and drop earrings are fabulous fauxs. Photo: Marili Forastieri.

🍂 (Opposite, right) Dazzling examples for a formal affair: The bracelet is worked in a lattice design; the clip-on earrings are classically shaped. The necklace would be elegant worn with a strapless gown. Photos: Iraida Icaza.

🍂 (Above) A lace ruffled "treasure box" for monetary gifts given to the bride at the reception is pictured beside bridesmaids' bouquets. Photo: Georgia Sheron.

🍂 (Right) Just the ideal size to hold bridal essentials, this satin clutch is gently touched with soutache and pearls. Bag: Dyeables. Photo: Marili Forastieri.

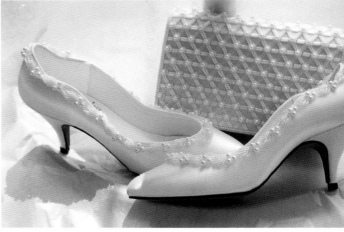

Fashion for the feet, from special shoes to sneakers.
🐝 (Left) Sequined clips add sparkle to satin pumps, pictured with other equally important accessories. Photo: Georgia Sheron.
🐝 (Above, left) Slipping into sneakers that may or may not be noticed beneath the bridal gown. Photo: Laurie Klein.
🐝 (Above) "And a coin in your shoe…" This contemporary satin style is dressed with a bow. And pumps traced with pearl details match a lustrous clutch bag. Photos: Georgia Sheron.
🐝 (Opposite) Glamorized canvas flats seemed the logical choice for this bride who loves to dance. Photo: Richard Fanning.

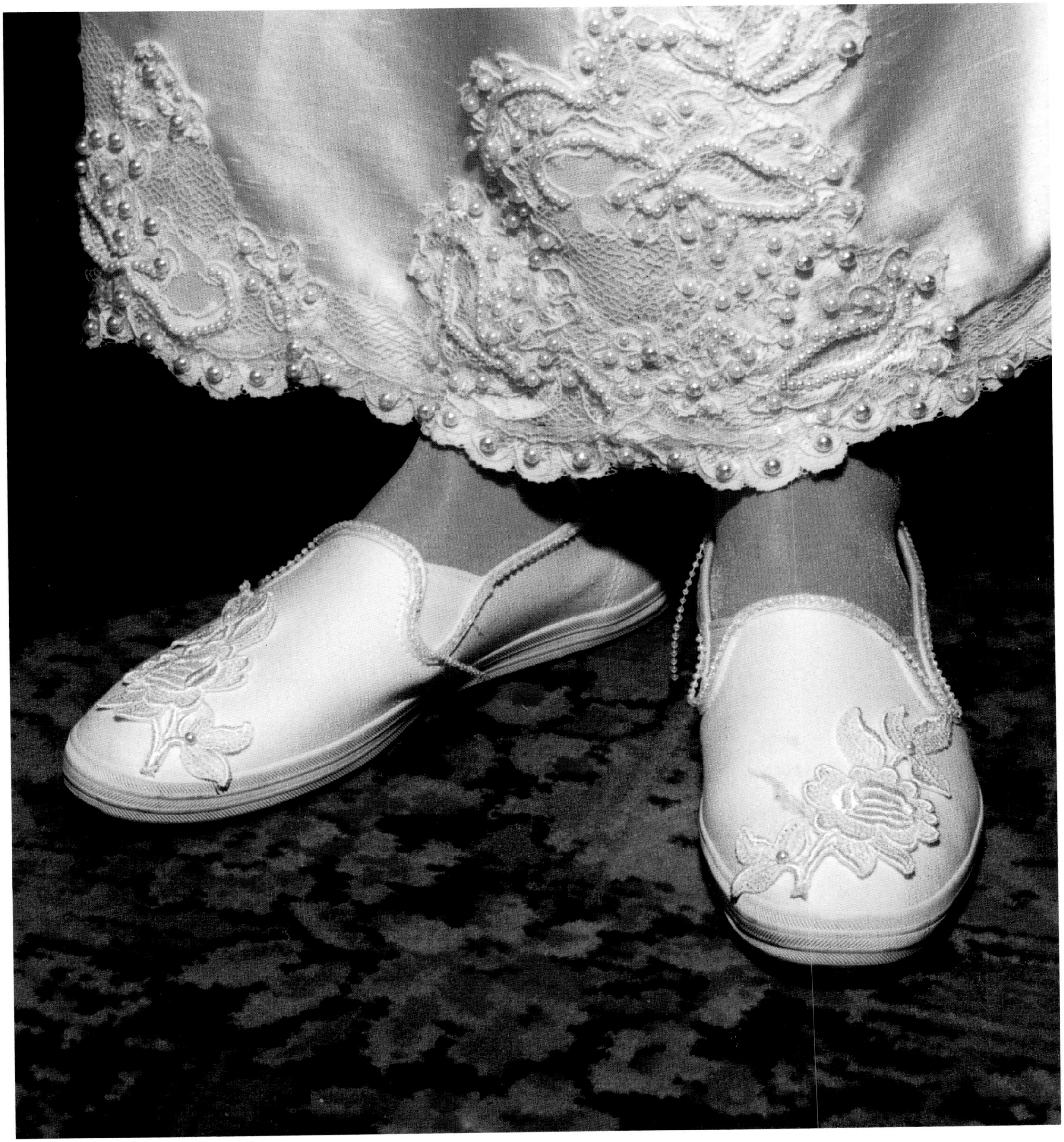

A breathtaking gown deserves to be matched with wedding shoes that possess wonderful silhouettes all their own. Choosing may be difficult, since the combinations of style and materials are imaginative. Available in a variety of heel heights, made of satin, silk, brocade or leather, and trimmed with lace, sequins, ribbons or bows, shoes are truly the finishing touch. All the sling backs and pumps shown on this page, and opposite, were designed by Stuart Weitzman. Photos: Courtesy of Stuart Weitzman.

A collection of contemporary wedding-day shoes, from modern to romantic.

🌺 (Opposite) A jeweled clip dresses a richly textured silk shoe. Photo: Iraida Icaza.

🌺 (This page) From designer Peter Fox, strappy sling backs, lace-up boots, fanned vamps, and crystal ornaments represent just a few of the innovative design elements available in bridal shoes. And, happily, many can be dyed and worn again after the wedding. Photos: Courtesy of Peter Fox Shoes.

~~~~~~

The little luxuries that add a special touch to the wedding are often handmade, given as gifts or passed down
as heirlooms to the bride and groom.

❧ (Opposite, left) An antique handkerchief and garnet, a symbol of good luck and good fortune, were
presented to the bride by her officiant.

❧ (Opposite, right, top) A "money bag," the softly adorned pouch used to hold monetary gifts at the reception.

❧ (Opposite, right, bottom) A frilly garter circled with picot-edged ribbon was custom made for a bride by the designer
of her wedding dress.

❧ (Above) This layered eyelet pillow may be used to cushion rings, boutonnieres or corsages.

All photos on this spread: Georgia Sheron.

~~~~~~

THE CEREMONY

hether it begins with a march down a church aisle, a cab ride to City Hall, a walk into a trellised garden, or a descent down your own staircase, a marriage ceremony will unite you and the person you love as husband and wife. Regardless of the setting you select, this event is a universal rite that signifies the beginning of a new life together.

(Preceding spread) This bride and groom exchange their vows before a breathtaking view in California's Napa Valley. The wine country has become a popular wedding site for many outdoor ceremonies. Photo: Jeff Meyers for Wine Country Weddings.

(Left) After their military wedding, this couple walks beneath crossed swords. Photo: Charlotte Maher.

(Opposite) A ceremony program can include the order of the service as well as personal notes of thanks. Photo: Dan Waggoner.

*T*he religious or civil service that you choose will establish the basic format of your wedding ceremony. Those elements that make a wedding ceremony unique, however, arise from the thoughts and emotions you and your groom choose to share with each other and with your guests and the ways you express these sentiments.

*W*riting part or all of your ceremony is one way to express your feelings. Personalized vows that reflect your commitment to each other must come from the heart, and your own words can reaffirm the themes of love, joy, fidelity, and respect that are so meaningful. As you prepare your vows, though, be sure to consult first with the officiant performing your service to determine which, if any, passages may be mandatory.

*Y*ou may want to have printed wedding programs that include important elements of your ceremony. As a keepsake as well as a guide, these programs can enhance the wedding for your guests by allowing them to follow the service more closely. The program may hold a note of thanks to parents, a description of a unique tradition, a prayer or quotation or poem, or a tribute to a deceased relative or friend. Standard information in a wedding program usually includes the wedding date, location, and time; the names of those in the wedding party; the officiant or co-celebrants; and any musicians or soloists and the titles of the music performed.

*T*he music you select for your wedding will set the tone for your ceremony from the prelude through the final joyous recessional. Whether you're planning to be married in a majestic church or at home or in a more unusual setting, choose music that is appropriate to your wedding environment.

*T*he grandeur of a trumpet flourish, the classic dignity of a church organ, or the charming simplicity of a soloist or string quartet—decide who will perform your wedding music, and surround yourself and your guests with the sounds you love. You may want to stay with the traditional—Lohengrin's "Bridal Chorus" and Mendelssohn's "Wedding March"—or possibly something lighter or more intimate. Love songs and ballads, even folk songs and movie themes, might be among your list of favorites. Your organist or a musical friend or family member can give you some suggestions, but be sure to clear your final choices with the officiant who will perform the ceremony.

~ THE WAYS WE WED ~

A wedding offers you and your fiancé the perfect opportunity to express yourselves, whether by incorporating a favorite interest or an unusual experience as a theme. For many couples, the object is to create an unforgettable day—in more ways than one.

(Left) Under a canopy of softly-lit ficus trees, this bride and groom exchange vows in a Jewish ceremony. Photo: Christine Newman.

(Opposite) Rock climbers forever! This groom's love knows no bounds as he climbs to join his bride high atop a scenic overlook. Photo: Richard Fanning.

When Jennifer and Russell Palmer began to plan their wedding, they knew no routine day would do. Lovers of all that's medieval, this Connecticut couple created a Renaissance event.

"*I*'ve always been infatuated with King Arthur's story and Celtic ancestry," says Jennifer, who also wanted a warm feeling for her November wedding. "We found an English Tudor manor complete with stone floors, stained-glass windows, and a stone hearth—it was ideal. An Elizabethan quartet played during our ceremony, which took place in the great hall. It was drizzling outside—even the weather was English—so we had a fire going. An old hymn was played for the processional and a bagpipe was played for the recessional. At the reception, the tables were arranged to form a large *U*, and candles ran the length of them. And, of course, our cake was in the shape of a castle."

*S*cience played a role in the courtship and marriage of Janet and Doug Hardy. She's a research scientist who studies snow, he's an Arctic hydrologist, and they met while on a glaciological research training program in Alaska. Although from different states—she from Colorado, he from Idaho—they dated and eventually both settled in California's Yosemite National Park. With summers off, Doug and Janet take on seasonal jobs during those months. One year, while Janet worked on Mount Olympus in Washington State, Doug paid a visit. The couple decided to marry while on Panic Peak!

*T*he wedding that followed took place at Taft Point, a panoramic spot some two thousand feet above Yosemite Valley. The couple and their one hundred guests walked one mile through a forest to reach the granite point. Janet wore a silk dress that Doug actually made for her; she sewed the vest for his outfit.

"The ceremony itself was simple," recalls Janet. "We basically wrote our own vows and had friends play the music. During the service, we asked the approval of all our guests, rather than just our parents. The response was lots of hoots and hollers, which made us feel just great. After the ceremony, everyone lingered at the point for awhile, eating chocolate and drinking fruit juice—we all needed energy for the long walk back!"

As director of public relations for the Four Seasons Hotel and Resort on Bali, Ilona Toth admires the gentle, spiritual ways of the island's natives. Thus she and her fiancé Gary Robinson decided to marry there. Ilona arrived in Hong Kong from the United States on a newspaper assignment and eventually made her way to Bali. While living in China, she met Gary, a native Londoner who was also working in Hong Kong. Their romance survived

Contrasting styles, each one truly memorable.

(Left) In this handsomely decorated hotel salon a band of tulle barred anyone from disturbing the beauty of the setting before the ceremony. Photo: Harold Hechler Associates, Ltd.

(Opposite) The cherished warmth of an at-home ceremony provides the most meaningful wedding environment for many couples. Photo: John Barber.

her move to the tropics, and while on one of his frequent visits to see Ilona, Gary proposed. And neither of them ever thought twice about where they would be wed.

"The Balinese people are very genuine, warm, and friendly—they love celebrations and festivals. And since they have so many rites of their own, they especially love the idea of marriage," says Ilona, who designed their handpainted wedding invitations, each one mailed in its own batik box. "Our ceremony took place at sunset on a hillside in Ubud, a well-known artist colony that overlooks the valley, river, and rice paddies. Traditional Balinese decorations—intricate palm-leaf weavework and magnificent orchids—were used all around. And a gamelan band, which is made up of bamboo instruments, played in the background. Everything was just perfect for us, and truly mystical."

Ruth Epstein, a justice of the peace living in Kent, Connecticut, has hiked, often literally, to some fairly unusual wedding sites in order to perform her duties. She explains, "One couple asked that I meet them at our town's noted covered bridge. They were cycling enthusiasts who loved to cross the bridge on bike trips. At the appointed hour on the wedding day, they arrived on their bicycles, we stopped traffic for several minutes for the marriage ceremony, and they cycled off on their honeymoon."

Even in a modern metropolis, some couples have unique ways of tying the knot. When Stacey Daniels and Cas Trapp, both floral designers in New York City, decided to marry, they had no way of knowing that the city's biggest blizzard in decades would hit on the same day as their March 1993 wedding. Naturally, they worried about whether their family, friends, and officiant would arrive not just on time, but at all. Somehow nearly every guest defied the odds and made it to the loft Stacey and Cas had chosen for their ceremony and reception. With the storm raging outside, the lushly decorated interior space looked especially romantic in contrast.

What do two floral designers choose for their wedding decor? "Tons of lilacs, verbinium, French tulips, Anna roses from the south of France, lisianthus, and daffodils," says Stacey, who did the planning herself but not the actual decorating. "Cas is from Holland, and his father and stepmother are also florists there. They did almost everything. Pink and red rose petals lined window ledges, bouquets with wired ribbons were carried on each service tray, blooming pear branches were placed on the floor around pedestals that held even more flowers. No two arrangements were alike; they were positioned on the floor all around the loft in different types of urns. The colors were very pale and cool: lavender, blues, soft yellow, blush pink, and a range of greens from light to dark all created this incredible environment. We brought an entire spring garden inside on a wildly snowy day."

Also taking inspiration from their work, Janis and George Obermeier let the sky be their limit. As owners of Natural Highs, a company that promotes drug-free ways to feel good, Janis and George took their marriage to new heights—in a hot air balloon.

No wedding is too small: This intimate marriage ceremony took place beneath the grand, imposing arches of the Cathedral of St. John the Divine, in New York City. Photo: G. Gregory Geiger.

"This is a second marriage for both of us, so we wanted to do something different," says George. "Because we had some family members who weren't able to ride in a balloon, the actual vows were exchanged while we were still on the ground. Then two balloons went up, one carrying Janis, myself, and our kids, the other with Janis's father and some friends. It was such a peaceful, serene experience. The only problem was that because the wind conditions had to be perfect, we couldn't invite guests to join us in the air since there

was no guarantee we would be able to lift off that day. And we had a wonderful reception on the ground with all of our friends and family one month later."

Billy Barrow was working in Florida as a diving instructor when Ruth Schrenzel signed up as one of his first students. When love bloomed, an underwater wedding seemed the obvious choice. "I grew up on the water and made my living on the water, so it was a natural decision," says Billy, who still teaches diving when he's not on duty as a Coral Gables police officer. The ceremony took place on the Key Largo Dry Rocks near a statue of Christ—a gift from Italian divers that is dedicated to the lost souls of the sea. "All the vows were written on slates," remembers Billy. "Ruth and I only had to check an 'I Do' box to make it official. Some of our guests were in the water with us; those who didn't dive watched from a glass-bottomed boat. This was also followed by a religious ceremony—on dry land."

Many of today's couples choose to marry far away from home, and no locale is more coveted than tropical Hawaii. Alicia Bay Laurel, the director of A Wedding Made in Paradise, based on the island of Maui, has coordinated hundreds of long-distance weddings for couples who seek the unusual and can't be there to plan the event.

"Some months I'll have as many as thirty weddings to work on," says Laurel, who regularly gets calls and letters from nearly every country—Singapore to Scotland. "I've planned a Jewish wedding for an Argentinian and Canadian couple, a ceremony for a Danish architect and his Chinese bride complete with canoe transportation, and an off-shore catamaran service officiated by a Samoan minister. But one of my favorites was the wedding on horseback of two grandparents—their grandchildren urged the union. The bride raised thoroughbreds and the groom was a horseshoer, so the mode of transportation was a logical one. The ceremony was performed high on a hillside overlooking the ocean. It just took your breath away."

Medieval music, "best dogs," balloons, cliffside vows, a marriage made in Bali, or even a lovely service in your own neighborhood. The wedding rite means something different to every couple who takes part in it. If you rely on your own creative ideas and the resources to accommodate them, few dreams need go unfulfilled.

The planning, the excitement, and the anticipation all come down to this moment.

🐝 *(Above, left) Happiness radiates from the faces of this bride and her father as they walk down the aisle arm in arm. Photo: Michael Kohl.*

🐝 *(Above, right) Standing before their officiant in a majestic church, this couple listens intently to the words of their marriage service. Photo: Michael Kohl.*

🐝 *(Left) At the wedding of Denise and Michael Oppizzi at The Octagon House in Irvington-on-Hudson, New York, all eyes are on the groom as he slips the ring on his bride's finger. Photo: Andrew French.*

🐝 *(Opposite) In the most serious of moments, a little laughter helps ease the tension. This bride may have forgotten her lines, but she inspires giggles all around. Photo: Phyllis L. Keenan.*

❧ (Above) The New York City loft where Stacey
Daniels and Cas Trapp would soon greet their wedding
guests glows against a snowy night sky with the light of
handmade papier-mâché chandeliers. Photo: Bentley
Meeker Lighting and Staging Inc.
❧ (Left) As their wedding got under way, the atmos-
phere was transformed by this stylishly romantic setting.
Photo: Leonard Lewis.

🌿 *(Right) A justice of the peace performs a simple wedding service for this bride and groom with witnesses in attendance. Photo: Maureen DeFries.*

🌿 *(Below) Newlyweds at last: Gold lamé draping and a sprinkling of rose petals line the aisle for this couple seen leaving their outdoor ceremony. Photo: Ortiz Photography.*

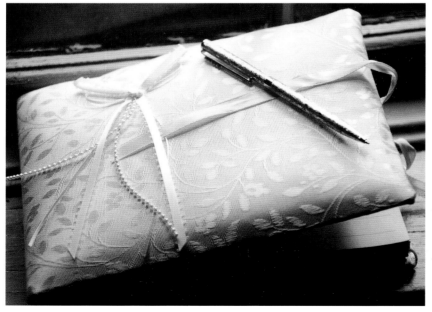

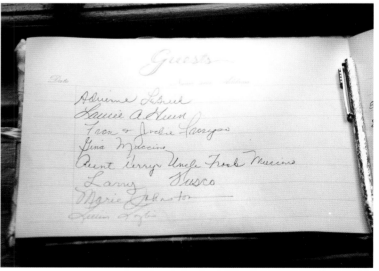

❧ *(Opposite, top) As a special keepsake, one couple requested signatures on the border of a print — "Wedding Morning," by John Bacon. Photo: Georgia Sheron.*

❧ *(Opposite, bottom) A ribbon-tied guest book collected the names of all invited. Photos: Georgia Sheron.*

❧ *(Right) The bride's bouquet, engagement ring, and wedding invitation form an elegant composition. Photo: Georgia Sheron.*

❧ *(Below) A beautiful wedding invitation printed in gold lettering and edged with a floral motif. This contemporary couple hosted their own affair.*

❧ *(Following page) Invitations and their enclosures can take any number of forms suited to the bride and groom's taste. Maps, sketches, verses, and even handmade batik envelopes have their place. Photo: Georgia Sheron.*

Nicolette Minozzi and Peter Teipel Murphy

invite you to join them in the celebration of their marriage

on Saturday, the twenty-first of August

nineteen hundred and ninety-three

at half after ten o'clock

St. Casimir's Church

239 Nepperhan Avenue, Yonkers, New York

WEDDING INVITATIONS

*B*efore you can visit a stationer to order invitations, you and your fiancé must know the number of guests you will be inviting to your wedding. Add at least twenty-five to your final count, as a margin for error; also include the number of invitations you would like to preserve as mementos.

*F*or a formal or semiformal affair, appropriate choices include white, ivory, or ecru stock paper printed by either the engraving or thermography processes. In engraving, the more costly of the two techniques, words are etched into a copper plate; its cavities are then filled with ink, and the paper is pressed into the plate. Thermography is created by a resinous powder that is melted over the flat-printed ink. Although both processes offer similar results, engraving still remains the choice of many traditionalists.

*I*t is best if you can place your order at least three months in advance; you may want to receive the mailing envelopes immediately so you can begin addressing them. Mail out-of-town invitations six weeks before the wedding, local invitations four weeks in advance.

*S*everal enclosures usually accompany the invitation. These days, a response card is generally included to make it easier for guests to reply. Some people prefer the time-honored courtesy of replying by handwritten note; in this situation, include the phrase "The favor of a reply is requested" on the reception card. The reception card also indicates the time and location of your reception, if it is being held at a site separate from your ceremony. And, including a map or suggestions for hotel accommodations for out-of-town guests is thoughtful and practical.

*T*o assemble the invitations, stack the papers in size order: invitation, tissue square (if provided), reception card, and reply envelope (with the card slipped under the flap). Place these into the inner envelope (don't seal it), then slip this packet into the mailing envelope, with the front of the inner envelope facing the back of the mailing envelope.

*C*onsidering today's many family arrangements and untraditional situations, you may need to consult a reliable etiquette book or a wedding planner about the appropriate wording for your invitation. Here is an example of a traditionally worded invitation for a wedding hosted by the bride's parents. (Both "honor" and "honour" are acceptable spellings, although the latter is more widely used.)

Mr. and Mrs. Brian Michael Roffman
request the honour of your presence
at the marriage of their daughter
Eve Lynn
to
Mr. Kevin Frederick Roberts
Saturday, the third of June
nineteen hundred and ninety-five
at two o'clock
St. Luke's Church
1800 Edwards Road
Alberta, New Hampshire

Memorable moments captured during Jewish ceremonies. (Left) A couple signs the ketubah, or marriage contract, in the presence of the rabbi and their families. Photo: Laurie Klein.
(Below) The bride and groom are blessed under a huppah on the Hawaiian island of Maui. Photo: Creative Touch Photography for A Wedding Made in Paradise.
(Opposite) Glorious rose topiaries line the aisle leading to a bride and groom exchanging vows under a floral arch. Photo: Harold Hechler Associates, Ltd.

Scenes at the altar.

🐚 (Left) Bridesmaids and groomsmen in attendance strike a neat symmetry. Photo: Nancy Muller, Rocky Mountain Images.

🐚 (Above, left) That most special exchange: A groom recites his marriage vows to his bride. Photo: Michael Kohl.

🐚 (Above, right) A father gives his daughter's hand in marriage. Photo: Dan Waggoner.

❧ *(Above) Well-wishers fill the church and watch while a unity candle is lit, a gesture symbolizing the joining together of the two families. Photo: Jonathan Farrer.*

❧ *(Left) Tears of joy: A lace hankie came in handy for this mother of the groom. Photo: Michael Kohl.*

Other countries, other traditions: Weddings the world over are marked by unique rituals.

❧ (Above) This Korean couple passes a red date between them, a symbol of fertility. Photo: Christine Newman.

❧ (Right) At this Hindu ceremony, a nuptial flame burns for Agni, the god of fire, in return for the blessings of prosperity, domestic happiness, and children. Photo: Marilyn Silverstone, © Magnum Photos.

🐚 (Above, left) Chandeliers and candlelight: At this Jewish wedding, black tie was the order of the day, and the elegant decor reflected the formality. Photo: Harold Hechler Associates, Ltd.

🐚 (Above, right) This bride and groom posed beneath a stained-glass icon after their traditional church wedding. Photo: Courtesy of Knott's Berry Farm.

Panoramic views and beautiful landscapes prompt many couples to marry in the great outdoors.

🐾 (Above) This couple married while on horseback with the Hawaiian island of Maui as their backdrop. The justice of the peace used the tailgate of his pick-up truck as an altar. Photo: Creative Touch Photography for A Wedding Made in Paradise.

🐾 (Left) The bridal party, including the "best dog," led this bride and groom to their scenic hilltop wedding site. Photos: left: Philip Grushkin; right: Michael Collopy.

≈ 110 ≈

⁂ *(Above and right) For a mountain-top wedding "out west," this bride arrived at the altar on horseback, but left on the arm of her husband. Photos: Above: Maureen DeFries. Right: Laurie Klein.*

For some couples, only the most unusual spots for a wedding will do.

🎞️ *(Opposite)* This bride and groom chose to be married midstream on a rocky little isle, surrounded by water. Photo: Richard Fanning.

🎞️ *(Above)* Swept off their feet: A pair of skydivers kissed as husband and wife surrounded by their airborne friends, thousands of feet above solid ground. Photo: Craig Hanson.

🎞️ *(Right)* Still others head under the sea: This scuba-diving couple exchanged their wedding bands well beneath the waves. Photo: The Waterhouse.

On the sea or in the air, getting there is half the fun.

🐚 (Opposite) These seafaring newlyweds embark on their latest adventure in their own sailboat. Photo: Maripat Goodwin Photography.

🐚 (Above, and top right) For this high-flying couple, vows were exchanged on the ground (so that all could attend), but their hot-air balloon took off soon afterwards. A second marriage for both the bride and groom, their children accompanied them on the ride. Photo: Frank Salomone/The Studio.

🐚 (Right, center and bottom) A canoe carried this Hawaiian bride to her exotic wedding, which took place in a typically tropical setting. Photos: David Vance for A Wedding Made in Paradise.

❧ *(Above and opposite)* *Setting out on their horses just before daybreak, this western bride and groom rode to their morning ceremony. After the wedding, they paused for a quiet moment beneath enormous trees at the site of nearby ruins. Photos: Fridrick Tiedemann.*

❧ *(Right)* *A horse-drawn carriage transports this couple and their honor attendants down a country lane. Photo: Laurie Klein.*

❧ *(Left, top and bottom) A glorious rainbow came out to bless this couple, who were wed aboard a catamaran in Hawaii. Photos: John Pierre for A Wedding Made in Paradise.*

❧ *(Above) What more dramatic background for this bride and groom's walk to their wedding site than the Colorado Rockies? Photo: Nancy Muller, Rocky Mountain Images.*

❧ *(Opposite) Roses, peonies, and ivy vines climb over the arch selected by this couple for their beautiful outdoor ceremony. Photo: Harrison Hurwitz.*

🐦 *(Opposite)* *To live out a fantasy, take a trip to Disney World. Cinderella's coach pulled by a team of white horses awaits this lucky bride. Photo: G. Gregory Geiger.*

🐦 *(Left)* *Inside the church, a bridesmaid keeps company with an adorable ring bearer and flower girl. Photo: Michael Kohl.*

🐦 *(Bottom)* *In a lovely natural wooded setting, guests welcome a cautiously approaching flower girl. Photo: Georgia Sheron.*

The bucolic charm of a country setting lends a refreshing simplicity to any wedding.

❧ *(Opposite) Viewed from above, this wedding landscape is punctuated by the long, white runner, bridesmaids all in pink, and a lone vegetable patch. Photo: Harold Hechler Associates, Ltd.*

❧ *(Above) A scene from long ago or from just yesterday? A timeless moment is captured as members of the bridal party pull away from a whitewashed country church in a horse-drawn carriage. Photo: Georgia Sheron.*

❧ *(Right) Wed on the Fourth of July, these newlyweds and their attendants fell right in step with the town's patriotic parade. Photo: Georgia Sheron.*

THE
FLOWERS

~

The beauty and symbolism of flowers lend a special meaning to many of the most important occasions in our lives. A fragrant bouquet or a colorful, carefully crafted arrangement of the freshest blossoms enhances any decoration scheme. Naturally, when it comes to your wedding celebration, the flowers you choose require careful consideration.

≈≈≈≈≈≈≈≈≈≈

(Preceding spread) Two bouquets in beautiful contrast: for the bride, roses, lilies, and Queen Anne's lace; her attendant will also carry roses, mixed with a variety of colorful blooms. Photo: Phyllis L. Keenan.

(Left) The splendid rose endures as the most popular flower for lovers. A full, round bouquet of roses makes a lasting impression and is still a favorite choice of brides. Flowers: Andrew Pasoe. Photo: Christine Newman.

≈≈≈≈≈≈≈≈≈≈

*I*n order to create a design, a florist needs to know certain facts about your wedding day: the ceremony and reception sites, the times of day, the style of your gown, and the color of your bridesmaids' dresses (it may help to have fabric swatches) are all essential elements to be considered. It is only natural to want your wedding festivities to be visually harmonious. Remember, though, this is *your* wedding, *your* day, so don't be afraid to express your own wishes, and to indicate to the florist how much or how little help you feel you need. Bring your florist to visit the ceremony and reception sites so that he or she can have a clear idea of what you envision. View the albums of past work and ask for suggestions and estimates within your budget. A true professional will take the time to understand your wishes and try to fulfill them.

*M*ost floral designers agree that a bride should arrive for a first meeting armed with lots of tear sheets from magazines showing examples of flowers she likes *and* dislikes. Tear sheets and photos help guide the florist to your specific tastes and the direction your wedding look will take.

*B*e sure to mention any flowers that have special meaning for you and your fiancé. If there was ever a time to surround yourselves with a favorite fragrance, color, and design, this is it. Some floral designers also suggest that you compose a list of appropriate adjectives describing what you would like to convey through the display flowers, even if you

~~~~~~~~~
☙ *Tall stems of white
and lavender delphini-
ums, casablanca lilies,
and sprigs of Queen
Anne's lace spring
from a glass bubble
vase at an outdoor
reception. Photo/
designer: Charles R.
Case.*
~~~~~~~~~

are not sure of the specific names of the blossoms. Such phrases as stark, linear, and clean; lush, full, and natural; colorful, fun, and happy; or romantic, soft, and light can often be more revealing than pictures.

Naturally your wishes are of primary importance, but there are two factors that help determine which flowers you might include in your wedding decorations. The first is the time of year you plan to marry. Most florists will advise that choosing seasonal flowers is wise. Not only does it make good economic sense (specially grown, imported flowers can be more expensive), but many brides prefer that the flowers decorating their wedding be representative of their region as well as the climate.

Although the rose, splendid in all its forms, remains the most popular of all wedding flowers throughout the year, there are dozens of other ideal seasonal choices. For spring celebrations, a beautiful selection of blooms may include bulbs (try tulips, anemones, ranunculus, and daffodils); sweet blossoms (peach, cherry, and apple); and an assortment of pussy willows, forsythia, heather, waxflowers, and roses. For summer through fall, some favorites are lilies, stephanotis, monte casino, and the many varieties of carnations. In the winter, many brides ask for all white flowers, such as roses, stephanotis, carnations, orchids, and gardenias—often with a touch of fragrant evergreens.

The second major factor that affects your floral scheme is the formality of your wedding. An outdoor celebration may call for bouquets and centerpieces with a "just-picked" look inspired by summer fields. But for a black tie event held in a hotel, you might want a more tailored view, perhaps flowers of all one color—crimson or lavender—set beside candelabras. However, don't hesitate to have what others might consider informal flowers at your formal celebration. Your first criteria should always be those blooms, or boughs, that reflect your vision and make you happy.

All the signs of a celebration: an elegant table setting, beautifully wrapped gifts, and, of course, fragrant flowers. Here, the romantic rose is featured in every wedding detail, from the bride's headpiece and bouquet to the artistic, towering centerpiece. Flowers: Elan Flowers. Photo: © 1991 Susan Wides.

~ THE BOUQUET ~

*F*resh flowers can enhance any chosen setting for either the ceremony or reception, but it is your bridal bouquet that often makes the most lasting impression. When it comes to choosing a shape, your florist may create any number of pleasing designs. There are three styles that remain most popular: the flowing *cascade bouquet*, the classic *nosegay*, and the graceful *arm bouquet*. Because each of these basic styles can, of course, be styled and modified to your liking, be sure to discuss your preferences with your floral designer.

*B*uttercups, lilacs, and lilies of the valley; roses, ranunculus, and bachelor's buttons; stephanotis, sweet peas, and forsythia—the limitless colors, combinations, and heady fragrances are easily translated into unforgettable arrangements by a floral designer. Your idea may be to create rich contrasts and dramatic shapes or delicate shades worked into neat nosegays. Together you and the florist can design a beautiful bouquet.

*C*olor can be incorporated into any aspect of floral decorations; however, many brides choose only white blooms for their own bouquets—and floral designer Virginia Wolff, owner of Virginia Wolff, Inc., of Chicago, couldn't be happier. "I don't believe in colored bride's bouquets because your eye immediately goes to the flowers. But the bride is

A single rose or lovely lily has a unique beauty. But when combined in a bouquet—with other blooms and greenery—the bright, colorful effect is simply spectacular. Photo: Jonathan Farrer.

A bridal bouquet of pale pink roses in full bloom is shaped into a gentle cascade. The roses are entwined with satin ribbons and ivy. Flowers: Vena Lefferts. Photo: Georgia Sheron.

the first thing you see if she is carrying a white, monochromatic bouquet that blends in with her dress—and that's the way it should be!"

*B*ig, white casablanca lilies in a cascade bouquet or the summery blend of Hawaiian dendrobium orchids are choices that make a strong statement. For something a bit more traditional, Wolff may combine white roses, stephanotis, and freesia; the last a particularly pleasing selection for the bride to carry "because freesia's long, skinny stems tend to tremble."

*I*f you're set on a touch of color, try a pastel composition: pale peach Osiana roses, pink phlox, irises in the softest lavender, and champagne roses are a few favorites for achieving a romantic look.

*A*ttendants' bouquets may be as colorful as you wish, and it's up to you whether the flowers you choose complement or contrast with the shade of their dresses. Do plan, though, to have the bouquets work with the rest of the wedding flowers, such as those used for centerpieces or the bows at the ends of church pews. Attention to these details will create unity and enhance the floral theme. For still more continuity, consider using the same type of flower in the attendants' bouquets as in the bride's bouquet. For instance, her creamy white roses may be complemented by roses in hot shades against deep velvet dresses or by roses in jewel tones with floral-print gowns.

*T*o add a more personal touch to the bouquet, you might want to provide your florist with ribbon or pieces of fabric that match your wedding gown or attendants' dresses to be incorporated into the design. And if you want to toss your bouquet but don't really want to part with it, request that a simpler bouquet be made just for this event. Extra long ribbon streamers tied around the stems make for a fabulous photograph as the bouquet sails towards waiting hands.

∼ THE CEREMONY ∼

The flowers and colors you choose for your wedding ceremony will depend a great deal on the style of the church or temple, home or garden, or whatever site you have chosen. In a religious setting, your choices should be both joyful and dignified to convey the feeling of celebration. Consider the scale and architectural details of the building's interior when deciding on altar and pew decorations. For example, in a large space, don't make the mistake of spreading your dollars too thin. Instead of several small arrangements on the altar and bows on every pew, opt for a single grand altar composition and decorations for the first few family pews.

Many florists agree that the simple use of color plays an important role in flowers for the ceremony. A fresh, lively palette may be needed for contrast in a dark, wood-filled

A magnificent alternative to potted arrangements or flower baskets at the ceremony, this pretty floral arch became a focal point in the church — and looks fabulous in photographs. Photo: Georgia Sheron.

space, while a more modern, well-lit setting would benefit from a number of schemes ranging from rich, jewel tones to classic all-white. In fact, even less expensive white flowers, such as gladiolas, generally look regal at a ceremony when used in full, lush arrangements.

An increase in formal, traditional weddings is being noted by florists all over the country, and some of the charm of such ceremonies comes from the presence of fresh-faced—and unpredictable—children. Flower girls look absolutely delightful carrying bouquets and tossing rose petals.

More inventive contemporary designs have evolved for the youngest members of the wedding, thanks to floral designers like David Kurio of Austin, Texas, who proposes, for example, that "if there are two children in the wedding, they can walk down the aisle each holding the end of a garland. That same garland can later be hung on the back of the bride's chair at the reception or across the guest-book table.

"In a Jewish ceremony, garlands can also be used to decorate the *huppah*, the canopy that symbolizes the couple's new home. Woven strands of lush flowers may trim the top edges and be entwined around the structure's poles. Another fresh idea is for flower girls to carry pomanders instead of bouquets. I've made them with stephanotis, roses, and alstromeria and hung them by wired French ribbon. If there are many children in the wedding, the girls could hold pomanders, and the boys could carry garlands."

The whole family carries flowers that echo the bride's bouquet. With the addition of daisies, the girls' bouquets are smaller versions of their mother's, a second-time bride. Photo: Maripat Goodwin Photography.

Creative florists strive for decorations with a difference. The unusual touches at a wedding are the most memorable, and designer Wolff welcomes the challenge to create such memories by improving upon standard floral ideas. "Flower girls look wonderful wearing wreaths on their heads," she says, "but instead of tiny buds, I like to make halos of big, floppy roses—it's much more adorable.

"Another old idea that's making a comeback are entry arches to the aisle in a church or hotel. Two large urns form the base at either side, and the arch springs up out of them. It's a very romantic addition to the ceremony."

～ THE RECEPTION ～

Decorating a reception site requires an eye for detail and an expert feel for color. Professional floral designers are able to transform your hall, club, or tent into precisely the space you envision—only lovelier.

Creativity has come to play an increasingly larger role at many wedding receptions. Happily, brides and grooms are contributing many more of their own ideas to help assemble a look that reflects their personalities. Recently, Wolff worked with a Jewish couple whose wedding took place in the fall, around the time of *Sukkoth*, the festival of the harvest. "To help represent their heritage, I used a variety of fruits and vegetables, such as peaches, lady apples, and cabbages, together with the flowers." The results were fabulous three-dimensional still-life paintings with an earthy scent.

A brilliant palette of purple and pink looks dramatic against this white table setting. The casual shape of the arrangement seems to have been styled effortlessly—the trademark of a truly talented floral designer. Photo: Maripat Goodwin Photography.

For weddings held from January through April, designer Kurio suggests filling tall glass vases with flowering branches from trees then in bloom, such as quince, forsythia, and dogwood. The towering branches look impressive, fill up a room, and are much more affordable than out-of-season blossoms.

Color is another consideration that greatly influences the overall look of your reception. Again, your florist should make recommendations to you based on the style and size of the space you've chosen. For evening weddings, a bit more drama and formality can be achieved with flowers in a single color. Kurio prefers this elegant, subdued look for parties held later in the day, whether he uses tones of white on white or a deep, rich red. Brides may, however, request a burst of color, especially when a light palette or pastels were used during the ceremony.

Garlands, those fragrant lengths of flowers and greenery that accent a ceremony in so many wonderful ways, may also enhance the points of interest at your reception. As the covering for a mantel, the valance atop a window, or the decoration surrounding a cake, gar-

lands highlight areas that might otherwise go unnoticed while helping to shape a more romantic environment. An ideal spot for a garland is around a banister. Other staircase decorations might include a full length of baby's breath, and a bouquet at the bottom with an ivy trail, or boughs of holly for a holiday wedding. While visiting the site you've chosen, your floral designer may notice other suitable spots for flowers, so be sure to ask for his or her ideas.

From delicate to dramatic, floral arrangements can add an enchanting element to your wedding, surrounding you with warmth, beauty and romance.

(Left) Since tradition is not every bride's choice, floral designers are continually creating unique options. This "bridal boa" for a bride dressed in basic black is an alternative to a bouquet and can be wrapped many ways. Photo: Elizabeth Ryan.

(Opposite) This wispy centerpiece of delicate flowers and grasses was inspired by ikebana, the Japanese art of flower arranging. Placed among pebbles and votives, these irises and hyacinths have an understated elegance. Flowers: Charles R. Case. Photo: Martin Jornallyay.

THE LANGUAGE OF FLOWERS

Alstromeria ~	Devotion
Aster ~	Symbol of love; daintiness
Azalea ~	"Take care of yourself for me"
Baby's breath ~	Pure heart
Bluebell ~	Humility
Calla lily ~	Beauty, elegance
Camellia ~	Admiration, good luck
Carnation ~	Lasting fidelity, deep love
Chrysanthemum ~	"You're a wonderful friend"; cheerfulness
Daffodil ~	Regard, joy, devotion
Daisy ~	Loyal love, faith, purity
Fern ~	Magic, fascination, beauty
Forget-me-not ~	True love, memories
Forsythia ~	Anticipation
Freesia ~	Innocence
Gardenia ~	"You're lovely"; joy
Gladiola ~	Generosity, beauty
Honeysuckle ~	Generous and devoted affection
Iris ~	Faith, friendship, wisdom
Ivy ~	Wedded love, fidelity, affection
Jonquil ~	"Love me"; desire
Lily of the valley ~	"You've made my life complete"; sweetness
Magnolia ~	Nobility
Myrtle ~	Love; Hebrew emblem of marriage
Orange blossom ~	Eternal love, marriage, fidelity
Orchid ~	Love, beauty, fertility
Peony ~	Happy marriage
Rose ~	Happy love, friendship
Rosebud ~	Beauty, youth, purity
Stephanotis ~	Happiness in marriage
Stock ~	Bonds of affection
Sweet pea ~	Blissful pleasure
Tulip ~	Perfect lover; fame
Violet ~	Modesty
Zinnia ~	Goodness, lasting affection

❦ (Opposite) Close-up of a bride's exquisite pastel bouquet. Flowers: Elan Flowers. Photo: (c)1991 Susan Wildes.

❦ (Below) A bride admires her bouquet, a varied arrangement of brightly colored flowers which has a garden-fresh feeling. Photo: Maureen DeFries for Laurie Klein Gallery.

❦ (Right) Many blooms carry symbolic meanings: the rose, which represents happy love and friendship, is still the favored flower for bridal bouquets. Here, large, creamy roses fall in a dramatic cascade. Photo/designer: Vena Lefferts.

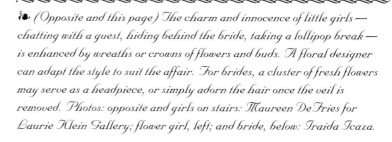

(Opposite and this page) The charm and innocence of little girls —
chatting with a guest, hiding behind the bride, taking a lollipop break —
is enhanced by wreaths or crowns of flowers and buds. A floral designer
can adapt the style to suit the affair. For brides, a cluster of fresh flowers
may serve as a headpiece, or simply adorn the hair once the veil is
removed. Photos: opposite and girls on stairs: Maureen DeFries for
Laurie Klein Gallery; flower girl, left; and bride, below: Iraida Icaza.

� *(Opposite, left) Naturally, every member of the wedding party needs flowers. A hand-tied bridesmaid's bouquet looks fresh picked from the meadow thanks to the creative use of wildflowers and leaves. Flowers: Vena Lefferts. Photo: Maureen DeFries for Laurie Klein Gallery.*

🌿 *(Opposite, right column) Fragrant corsages adorn the shoulders or wrists of mothers and grandmothers of the bride and groom, or other honored guests. Boutonnieres for dads, the groom, and his party may range from a single rose to a more expressive design. From top: photo/designer: Vena Lefferts; Vena Lefferts; Georgia Sheron.*

🌿 *(Above) A pair of bridesmaids' bouquets resting on chairs creates a pretty still life. Lush peach and ivory stock, pale blue delphiniums, and white, coral, and peach roses give these bouquets the luminous look of a watercolor. Flowers: Charles R. Case. Photo: G. Gregory Geiger.*

❧ *(Opposite) Dewy Bridal Pink roses, green vibur-*
num, purple stock, and lavender sweet peas are tied in a
natural shape with white satin ribbon. Flowers:
Charles R. Case. Photo: G. Gregory Geiger.
❧ *(Below) As befits a flower girl, this demure*
bouquet of miniature garden roses is framed by a soft
collar of Queen Anne's lace. Flowers: Diane Jamison
Personal Flowers. Photo: Marili Forastieri.
❧ *(Right) Simply elegant, calla lilies combined with*
a slender grass are a sophisticated choice for a bridal
bouquet. The long stems look wonderful when braided
with special ribbons. Designer: All About Flowers.
Photo: Georgia Sheron.

❧ *(Left) A lacy bow highlights the soft shape of this rose bouquet mixed with lily-of-the-valley sprigs. Flowers: Charles R. Case. Photo: G. Gregory Geiger.*

❧ *(Below) A bouquet of deep orange parrot tulips, peach calla lilies, and scotch broom is wrapped with rich gold and pink ribbons. Flowers: Diane Jamison Personal Flowers. Photo: Otero.*

❧ *(Inset) A bouquet of pale pink roses is tied with wired silver metallic ribbons that seem to float in the breeze. Flowers: Vena Lefferts. Photo: Maureen DeFries for Laurie Klein Gallery.*

🌢 *(Above, left) A white cascade bouquet combines roses with stems of stephanotis and Hawaiian dendrobium orchids. Flowers: Charles R. Case. Photo: G. Gregory Geiger.*

🌢 *(Above) Tulip bouquets for the bride and her attendant are tied with exquisite tapestry ribbons. Flowers: Diane Jamison Personal Flowers. Photo: Otero.*

🌹 *(Opposite) Regal calla lilies, tinged with pink, stand out in a white bouquet finished with long, feathery ferns and grasses. Photo: Iraida Icaza.*

🌹 *(This page) For traditional all-white bouquets, a lush, romantic look can be created using only a few blooms. These are three beautiful examples: white Dutch irises (left, top); white dahlias and ivy (left, bottom); and Bridal white roses and gardenias (right). Flowers: Diane Jamison Personal Flowers. Photos: George Holz.*

🌺 *(Opposite) Topiaries make ideal centerpieces: their tall, slender shapes are set in containers and burst into flowers and greenery within view of all the guests. Graceful, flowing streamers descend to the table from this ribbon and rose topiary. Flowers: All About Flowers. Photo: Georgia Sheron.*

🌺 *(Below) The same topiary is shown in reception surroundings—the focal point amidst a pure white table setting.*

🌺 *(Right) A medley of red, white, and green covers a sphere that is set into a classical urn. Flowers by Renny. Photo: Emily Miller.*

❧ *(Top left) Beside the fireplace at a stately reception, a pot overflows with a burst of white, including French tulips, snapdragons, and dogwood branches. A single color, mixed with greenery, can make an elegant statement. Flowers: Charles R. Case. Photo: G. Gregory Geiger.*

❧ *(Bottom left) A basket brimming with colorful wildflowers brightens up a space featuring marble and wood. Photo: Stephane Colbert.*

❧ *(Below) At home, a vase filled with long-stemmed purple allium, mock orange blossoms, peonies, lilies, and snapdragons complements the room's striking color scheme. Flowers: Charles R. Case. Photo: G. Gregory Geiger.*

❧ *(Opposite) A magnificent display packed tight with an assortment featuring roses, French tulips, heather, statice and stock, greets guests as they enter the reception. Flowers: Charles R. Case. Photo: G. Gregory Geiger.*

✿ (Above) A centerpiece of flowers in soft pastels looks romantic on a table set in all white. Photo/designer: Vena Lefferts.

✿ (Left) On the patio of The Dairy in New York City's Central Park, jewel-tone flowers in centerpieces and hanging baskets look striking against green lawns and trees. Flowers: Paul Bott. Photo: Courtesy of Moveable Feast.

✿ (Below, left) Junior bridesmaids carry classic little nosegays of pink and cream roses. Photo/designer: Vena Lefferts.

✿ (Below, right) French garden roses and stock—a fragrant centerpiece mix surrounded by extra-tall tapers. Photo/designer: Charles R. Case.

✿ (Opposite) The centerpieces for a grand ballroom must be generous in order to be seen. Here, tall glass vases hold arrangements featuring stargazer lilies. Trees strung with soft white lights are placed around the room to fill in empty spaces. Photo: Harold Hechler Associates, Ltd.

(Above) The creative floral designer will match colorful tablecloths with complementary centerpieces. These three photographs display distinctive, delightful uses of color and texture. Peonies, stock, irises, and delphiniums were combined (above, left); lilac, peonies, stock, roses, and delphiniums (upper, right); and graceful lilies of the valley (lower, right). Flowers: Charles R. Case. Photos: G. Gregory Geiger.

(Left) There are scarcely two flowers alike in this centerpiece that makes use of a wide variety of blooms. The silver basket is the ideal showcase for so much subtle color. Flowers: Charles R. Case. Photo: Martin Tornallyay.

(Above) Votive candles placed inside miniature bird's nests help illuminate this lovely landscape of spring flowers—perfect for use on a buffet or head reception table. Some of the flowers included here are yellow and orange poppies, Queen Anne's lace, maidenhair fern, tangerine and yellow miniature gerbera daisies, and grape hyacinths. Flowers: Charles R. Case. Photo: Nancy McFarland.

(Right) A handful of pink gerbera daisies gives the stylized setting of this Japanese ikebana-style arrangement a pretty focus. Flowers: Charles R. Case. Photo: Martin Tornallyay.

🍃 (Opposite) A white trellis arch, dressed with flowers, greenery, and a satin bow, points the way to the wedding. Photo/designer: Charles R. Case.

🍃 (Above) This basket filled with pink and red flowers looks particularly delicate in an outdoor setting, such as atop this rustic stone wall. Photo: Phyllis L. Keenan.

🍃 (Right, top) Whether at a country church ceremony or an at-home reception, let the beauty of flowers welcome your guests. A simple cluster of flowers and leaves, paired with a floppy bow, spruces up this white picket fence. Photo: Vena Lefferts.

🍃 (Right, bottom) Pink and white peonies are tucked among feathery ferns to adorn a trellis that became the focus of a garden wedding. Flowers: Charles R. Case. Photo: G. Gregory Geiger.

(Left, top) Done in a palette of pink and white, this arrangement features silk roses and lilies among twisting vines of ivy and graces the center hall of a home preparing for a daytime wedding. Photo: Stephane Colbert.

(Left, bottom) A dramatic contrast: a sterling bowl filled with white lilies, stock and Lady Di roses has an air of elegance centered on a dark mahogany table. Flowers: Charles R. Case. Photo: G. Gregory Geiger.

(Below) A creative use of soft color fashions a charming touch at home: Italian carnations are grouped with Queen Anne's lace and tied in bunches with raffia bows. Flowers: Charles R. Case. Photo: G. Gregory Geiger.

❧ *(Above, left) The graceful style of ikebana, the Japanese art of flower arranging, inspired this design: a combination of ranunculus in shades of pink, tall green ixia, lavender freesia, and miniature agapanthus. Flowers: Charles R. Case. Photo: Nancy McFarland.*

❧ *(Above, right) When dried, flowers take on a new beauty. This large, colorful basket composition suits a country wedding setting perfectly. Photo: Stéphane Colbert.*

❧ *(Right) A trio of tinted Mason jars gives an informal arrangement a unique look full of appeal. From left: Pink evening primroses and bachelor buttons, irises and yellow yarrow, and dark blue delphiniums with yellow freesias all look as if they were just clipped from the garden. Flowers: Charles R. Case. Photo: G. Gregory Geiger.*

THE RECEPTION

*I*t's the party of a lifetime. Your wedding reception celebrates your marriage, pampers your guests, and marks the glorious culmination of months of planning. The tone of the party will be largely determined by your own personal style as well as where you hold it and what you serve. The possibilities are exciting and varied, and the sky may often be the limit.

(Preceding spread) As night falls, this trellis-like interior is festively lit for a reception. Photo: Harold Hechler Associates, Ltd.

(Left) Limos by land, but boat by sea, this bride and groom docked right at their waterside reception site. Photo: Maripat Goodwin Photography.

~ Sites ~

In recent years, traditional wedding plans have been altered to fit more contemporary needs. On average, brides and grooms are now several years older and generally more sophisticated than their counterparts of fifty years ago. Although it has been customary for the bride's family to host the reception, many dual-career couples now pay for all or part of their wedding celebration.

These changes in lifestyles and personal tastes go hand in hand with the refreshing trend toward less traditional wedding sites. The recent roster of new and interesting wedding locales includes yachts, gardens, mansions, museums and art galleries, zoos, fairgrounds, bed-and-breakfast inns, movie studio lots, wineries—and, of course, the fantasy capital of the country, Disney World.

Whatever site you are considering, it's a good idea to visit—if at all possible, when another wedding is taking place there. While there, request a sample meal from the caterer, take a tour of the kitchen, and inspect the restrooms; a careful look at all the facilities is essential to hosting a happy and trouble-free party yourselves.

Having a wedding at home—yours or your parents' or a friend's—is another wonderful option, providing there is ample space. Marrying in a place that holds many special memories can be a pleasurable alternative to a rental site. Although the romance of this idea may seem irresistible, there are many factors to contemplate before you commit to it. First, consider that it's likely that your home

Majestic mirrors reflect the light in a stately mansion with remarkable detailing. Photo: Ronald J. Krowne. Courtesy Culinary Catering.

won't have the parking spaces, restroom facilities, or electrical capabilities needed to accommodate a large crowd. And providing these may prove to be a costly and logistical problem. Hiring your own caterer and decorator to furnish a site may be the choice of many who are prepared to pay, but this prospect can be surprisingly complicated. Careful planning—and perhaps the services of a wedding coordinator—are recommended for those whose hearts are set on an at-home reception.

*A*s wedding fêtes grow grander and guest lists grow longer, more and more brides and grooms are turning to hotels with spacious accommodations. When you book a hotel reception, the essential services are already in place. In addition to a chef, of course, a staff florist and bridal coordinator are usually available to you. Out-of-town guests may also reserve rooms in the hotel, usually at special rates. And some even offer their bridal suite to newlyweds for the wedding night as part of an arranged package. Even if the hotel you select for your reception offers all these services, you are not necessarily compelled to use them. If you have a favorite florist and caterer, it may be possible to hire them instead. Speak with the hotel representative about your preferences.

～ FOOD ～

*T*exans love a barbecue, New Yorkers savor the sit-down dinner. In between, the menu options are endless. An hors d'ouevres buffet, beach clambake, dessert reception, champagne brunch, cocktail dinner buffet, afternoon tea or garden luncheon have all served as appropriate wedding parties.

*R*egardless of the format you choose, beautiful tables and an elegant menu seem to result almost effortlessly when an experienced caterer unleashes his or her talents and love of good food. Spring and summer receptions can benefit from the bounty of the freshest produce and flavors of the season. For fall and winter, heartier fare that warms and comforts makes a fitting menu. And, of course, almost anything you want can be obtained at any time of year—if you are willing to pay for it.

*A*n open exchange of menu ideas with your caterer is very important: discuss everything from hors d'ouevres to desserts. Share your preferences, and learn about his or her favorite seasonal choices and signature recipes. Talk about your tastes and ethnic back-

On the menu at this outdoor reception, an icy raw bar offered the freshest of shellfish. Photo: Courtesy of Glorious Food.

grounds, in order to tailor a more personalized event through the food you serve. Also, first ask your caterer to visit your reception site since many of today's more unique locations may not have all the kitchen facilities necessary to prepare certain menus.

Consider the elements of the bar as well, and what constitutes an appropriate amount and type of liquor for your reception. The right number of champagne bottles should be ready to pour, and complementary dinner wines served at the proper times. A good caterer will also know how much liquor will be needed according to changes in the seasons (more Scotch is drunk in winter months, and vodka or gin in the summer, for example).

Having coordinated and cooked for an endless variety of weddings, Thomas Preti, owner of Thomas Preti Catering, a Westchester County, New York, company, has worked to fulfill many challenging wishes. A request for a Phantom of the Opera theme

---

LIGHT NONALCOHOLIC BEVERAGES
～

A cup of cheer — without the alcohol — is an increasingly welcome addition to many wedding celebrations. More health conscious guests are consuming less alcohol these days, making it necessary to offer other thirst-quenching options.

One such alternative is a water bar, stocked with the wet stuff in all its newest forms. Include the sparkling, mineral, fruit-flavored, and spring varieties. Add seltzer, club soda, and tonic water for extra fizz. Sparkling Water Distributors in Long Island City, New York, will even supply water in bottles with personalized wedding labels.

Besides water, beverage requests include sparkling cider (a suitable champagne stand-in for toasting) and other bubbly fruit juices. Today, it's also quite acceptable to serve frozen blender drinks without the alcohol. Margaritas still have zing sans tequila, and piña coladas taste tropical even without the rum.

Cool, colorful punch is another wonderful alternative to the usual assortment of reception drinks. Fresh and fruity, punch recipes are especially perfect for summer weddings and bridal showers.

There is also a compromise for those who prefer something stronger than water, but lighter than hard liquor. A white bar offers wine, champagne, and mixed vodka, gin, and rum drinks. For afternoon or brunch receptions, you might offer guests crystal cups of champagne punch during the cocktail hour. It's an elegant — and economical — change from an open bar.

A holiday-time reception can reflect the spirit of the season. Warm, rich colors, fragrant evergreens, festive decorations, and a hearty menu are the hallmarks of this wintertime wedding party. Photo: Jeremy Samuelson.

resulted in a black and white setting, from flowers to decorations. Miniature gold masks became part of the centerpieces and circled the base of the wedding cake.

Another celebration took place in a Connecticut museum filled with the largest collection of turn-of-the-century circus and arcade memorabilia, with the wedding decor reflecting this whimsical assortment. And one bride's lifelong desire to be married on her family's farm provided the setting for an informal yet festive wedding feast of a different sort. The message is you are no longer confined to simply follow tradition. You can shape your wedding to reflect your own personal style and taste — your own dream.

Naturally, a large part of that dream focuses on food. For many couples, weddings offer an opportunity to display pride in their heritages, and the menu serves as the mirror to their ethnic origins.

A meal including an eclectic blend of international foods is a common request heard by many caterers. Among Preti's clients, dozens of countries have been honored through a delicious sampling of national dishes. "For one Spanish wedding, we served a traditional *tapas* buffet and veal meatballs in a Chorizo sausage sauce. At a Middle Eastern mar-riage, there was roast lamb and couscous. We've made our own dim sum and dumplings for Asian parties and wursts and krauts for German ones. On the menu at a recent Italian wed-ding was porcini-filled, agnolotti pasta with prosciutto cream sauce served in a pastry shell."

At Ilona Toth and Gary Robinson's Balinesian wedding, they treated guests to a traditional Indonesian "night market" on the eve of their ceremony. Food stalls that featured roast pig, noodles, and fresh fruit showcased some of the island's favorite fare.

For Hawaiians, a luau is the way to celebrate. According to Alicia Bay Laurel of A Wedding Made in Paradise, Hawaiian buffets offer Polynesian specialties such as Kalua pig (baked in an underground oven), chicken long rice (actually a rice noodle), poi (ferment-ed taro root paste), Lomi salmon (a saladlike dish), and often a teriyaki. The region's tradi-tional dessert is *haupia*, a coconut pudding. For a twist, contemporary couples often ask for haupia to be used as the filling in their wedding cake.

Of course, more routine menus are still being served and savored by wedding guests everywhere. It's nice to know, though, that so many palates can be satisfied by gifted, expressive chefs.

〜 DECOR 〜

A reception room is basically a blank stage that is waiting to be transformed by flowers, lighting, and props. Depending upon the time and resources available, many brides choose to take on the task themselves. Others leave it to a floral designer or wedding consultant. Remember that whoever decorates the space that you have chosen should possess an eye for detail and a rich imagination.

Keep in mind that some locations may cry out for a specific theme, while others require more work and inspiration. Thanks to the amazing variety of party goods that can often be rented, everything from linens and lights to gazebos and greenery are available to bring an image to life.

Wedding consultants will help you to plan almost any size reception, performing a varying list of duties for newly engaged couples. And those professionals who oversee the event from start to finish are generally capable of working magic with any given decor.

At San Francisco's June Wedding, Inc., Robbi Ernst does just that, with a bit of guidance from the bride and groom. "When I look at a bare room, I first consider decorating the walls, then work inward," says Ernst, who gives clients a monthly computer readout of their checklist. "Ideas start to fall into place once the theme takes over, but there are certain rules that always apply. Lighting is the first, since it adds a dimension like nothing else can. Linens are another: you must have cloths down to the floor and use overlays for depth."

$\mathcal{W}$hen Virginia Gibson and Edward Burmeister, attorneys with the same law firm, set their wedding date, they wasted no time placing a call to Ernst. "Our wedding was full of elaborate details, and he was just the person to handle them," says Gibson.

$\mathcal{T}$he reception at San Francisco's Academy of Sciences in Golden Gate Park required careful planning because of the potential for so many creative tie-ins. For instance, during cocktails in the aquarium, sushi was served on silver trays. A sit-down dinner fol-

lowed in the African room of the Natural History Museum. Against the backdrop of elegant architecture and exotic animals, zebra-patterned tablecloths and leafy palms turned one exhibit hall into a wondrous safari setting.

$\mathcal{A}$nd the event ran like clockwork with Ernst at the helm. "He developed a game plan for the entire wedding day and was only off by ten minutes at the end," remembers Gibson. "The choreography of the evening was planned out in exacting detail."

$\mathcal{I}$n addition to professional party planners and bridal experts, the florist you hire to fill your day with fresh blooms may be experienced in decorating as well. "Floral designers should give you a lot of advice on many different facets, from flowers and plants to lighting and tablecloths," says Denise Oppizzi, who, with her husband, operates Michael Oppizzi & Co. in New York City. This design team prefers to create lush, dramatic floral statements rather than accenting a room with many smaller arrangements. The

$\mathcal{W}$hat kind of music is appropriate for a wedding reception? Everything from a string quartet to a 10-piece band, depending upon the tone of the party. These newlyweds danced to a faster beat. Photo: Ellis-Taylor Photographers.

Oppizzis also collect antique vases and containers for their business, making it possible for each table to have a unique centerpiece composed of different flowers and colors.

"Lighting is critical in order to create something magical, something fun," notes Michael Oppizzi. "It's needed to highlight or accent flowers, even if candlelight is used on

DANCE TO THE MUSIC

Unlike the more formal music traditional for the wedding ceremony, the song list you select for your reception will be romantic, festive, and fun. If your party is small, a jazz ensemble or pianist may be just the thing. For a larger celebration, a band or orchestra is a better choice for entertaining your guests. Or, if you have the space and budget, hire both groups to play in separate rooms—then there will surely be something for everyone.

A good band will be able to play a range of music that spans the decades, from Big Band standards to Top 40 to Motown hits, as well as ethnic pieces. If you have something specific in mind, share your ideas with the bandleader—he or she will very likely be able to accommodate almost any request. As an alternative to a live band, you might consider hiring a disc jockey as a cost-cutting measure. With the advent of the compact disc, you can feel confident that you'll hear high-quality sound. Also, depending upon the disc jockey's library, any number of songs can be played—or you might supply a few of your own favorite tunes on tape.

Specially chosen songs can be played to accompany several traditional reception highlights, such as the couple's first dance or the bride's dance with her father. If you have difficulty choosing an appropriate song, your bandleader will certainly be able to make suggestions or provide you with a lengthy list of ideas.

Lester Lanin, New York City's renowned bandleader extraordinaire, regularly tracks his most-requested reception melodies. Broadway show tunes and contemporary hits enjoy a block of time on his list, but some perennial favorites are rarely replaced. A few notable classics with staying power are "Rock Around the Clock," "It Had To Be You," "Unforgettable," "In The Mood," "Just In Time," "Embraceable You," and "Moonlight Serenade." Don't feel limited by what is popular, of course. The songs you choose may even start a new tradition.

the table. Even outdoors, lighting can be designed in creative ways. For instance, hanging a string of Japanese rice paper–lanterns can indicate where the food is being served. Column candles set in glass hurricanes that are placed around the grounds can give a sense of depth and romance. And the color of the lights can be used to set the tone of the reception as well."

For the Oppizzi's own September wedding at The Octagon House, a nineteenth-century mansion in Irvington-on-Hudson, New York, guests were seated outdoors at one continuous table that wrapped around four of the building's eight sides. The other four sides provided space for the ceremony, dancing, and the dessert table.

The unusual layout gave this clever couple the opportunity to be truly creative. "By having one long table we were able to use many types of centerpieces, from candelabras to antique vases filled with garden roses," says Michael. "We wanted to complement the beauty of the house. And since the party was held outside, we strived for a natural fall look using rich shades of orange, red, fuchsia, and yellow. Even the design and execution of the specially constructed tablecloth took two weeks—it was trimmed with swags and handmade rosettes."

(Left) For the wedding reception of floral designers Michael and Denise Oppizzi, richly set tables followed the curves of this splendid porch at The Octagon House in Irvington-on-Hudson, New York. Photo: Andrew French.

(Opposite) One of the oldest of wedding traditions: this new bride tosses her bouquet to friends. Photo: Jeff Meyers.

~ MORE PARTY NOTES ~

Traditionally, the wedding reception opens with a *receiving line*. The newlyweds and chosen members of the bridal party greet guests as they enter the site. Some couples, however, choose to assemble the line and receive congratulations immediately after the ceremony itself,

as guests file out. At an informal wedding, the couple may forego the line completely and simply circulate among friends and relatives, spending time with each.

As the celebration draws to an end, the bride and groom take their leave, which usually signals that it is time for guests to begin to leave. Often, the festivities do not end here, however. *Post-reception parties* are a popular way to extend the wedding and are also welcomed events for weekend guests who have traveled a good distance. For instance, an informal day-after breakfast, brunch, picnic, or barbecue, often hosted by a close friend or relative of the bride and groom, is a perfect ending to the celebration.

Clearly, a limousine is not the only way to travel to and from the reception.
❧ (Above, left) City lights and taxi cabs are always ready to point the way when you wed in a bustling metropolis. Photo: Laurie Klein.
❧ (Above, right) It's not San Francisco, but this trolley-for-hire didn't need tracks to carry off this couple. Photo: Richard Fanning.
❧ (Left) A festive basket of tulle-wrapped bunches of rose petals are ready for the guests to toss on the newlyweds as they leave the reception by whatever means. Photo: Georgia Sheron.

❧ *(Above) This wedding party personalized a pick-up truck for the bride and groom's getaway. Photo: Maureen DeFries.*

❧ *(Right) The party's over for these newlyweds who head off in a shower of flying rice. Photo: Maureen DeFries for Laurie Klein Gallery.*

A peek at meticulously arranged rooms, just before the marriage celebrations begin.

❧ (Left) The guests of honor sign their memory book as they arrive at
the reception. Photo: Maripat Goodwin Photography.

❧ (Above) Formally set tables and towering, spotlighted centerpieces
suit the grand architecture of this hotel ballroom. Photo: Harold
Hechler Associates, Ltd.

❧ (Opposite) An enclosed rooftop terrace becomes a plentiful garden
when a floral theme prevails, right down to the seat cushions. Photo:
Harold Hechler Associates, Ltd.

Reception

Two different receptions, two very different perspectives.

🔔 (Above) A close-up of the festivities, as the newlyweds kick off the dancing. Photo: Jonathan Farrer.

🔔 (Opposite) Viewed from a balcony, marvelous lighting created a dramatic atmosphere at a site on New York's Ellis Island. Spotlights that focused on the vaulted ceiling, tabletops, dance floor, and flags helped illuminate this room in a magical way. Photo: Bentley Meeker Lighting and Staging, Inc.

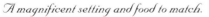

A magnificent setting and food to match.

❧ (Opposite) Luxurious surroundings enhanced by perfectly draped fabrics, covered chairs, and an abundance of candlelight transformed this tent into a marvel of design.

❧ (This page) From the kitchens of Glorious Food caterers in New York City, these delectable desserts include rows of fresh figs with berries, a holiday display complete with a towering croquembouche (meaning "crunch in the mouth"), a mound of cream puffs held together with a caramel glaze and trays of berries with a choice of sauces. All photos: Glorious Food.

Wedding receptions at waterside.
🎀 (Left) For this bride and groom, the ideal dance floor was right alongside the dock. Photo: Maripat Goodwin Photography.

🎀 *(Below, left) A drifting fog lent a misty mood to this poolside party. Photo: Georgia Sheron.*

🎀 *(Top, left) A fallen tree at the water's edge made a striking prop for the tuxedoed members of the wedding. Photo: Fridrick Tiedemann.*

🎀 *(Below) A luxurious yacht awaits the wedding guests. Photo: Maripat Goodwin Photography.*

(Top left) A night-time reception held under a tent glows with candelabras and tiny white lights. Photo: P. Melville for Culinary Architect Catering.

(Bottom left) A holiday wedding theme made wonderful use of seasonal decorations. Photo: Bernard Vidal.

(Opposite) Making a grand impression: A Christmas tree with twinkling lights, a wreath dressed with golden bows and velvet fruits, and a mantel draped with greenery, pomegranates, and pine cones. Flowers: Castle & Pierpont. Photo: Jeremy Samuelson.

🍂 *(Left) A Norwegian groom in his country's traditional wedding attire. Photo: Phyllis L. Keenan.*

🍂 *(Above) During an at-home reception, the bride and groom chat with their smallest guest on the front porch steps. Photo: Phyllis L. Keenan.*

🍂 *(Opposite) In northern California's wine country, many vineyards make their grounds available for weddings and receptions. One party (top) celebrated right beside a young crop. At another (bottom), guests were seated in the cavelike setting of a wine cellar. Photos: Bill Stockwell for Wine Country Weddings.*

Locales, cultures, and holidays are natural springboards for traditions and themes.

❧ (Opposite) For a reception held in the Natural History Museum at San Francisco's Academy of Sciences, a safari setting was inspired by the animals on display in the African room. Photo: June Weddings, Inc.

❧ (Below) In keeping with Jewish tradition, the bride and groom are lifted on chairs by their guests. Photo: Georgia Sheron.

❧ (Right) Feathery masks were only some of the treats at this Halloween day wedding. Photo: Craig Merrill.

❧ (Below, right) A close-up of the exotically masked bride and groom. Photo: Jerry Trafficanda.

With nature as the backdrop, an outdoor reception has beauty built in. ❧ (Opposite) A toast to happiness in a majestic botanical garden. Photo: Bernard Vidal. ❧ (Right) A swimming pool, shaded grounds, and a tent created a cool setting for this at-home summertime reception. Photo: Charles R. Case. ❧ (Bottom, right) Under this white tent, a splendid oasis appeared in the center of a great lawn. Photo: Courtesy of Glorious Food.

🌺 *(Left) A party of two: For these newlyweds, a private celebration, a country field, and a lovely meal was all that was needed. Photo: Laurie Klein.*

🌺 *(Above) A string quartet echoes the beauty of this picturesque wedding site. Photo: G. Gregory Geiger.*

🌺 *(Opposite) A casually-chic wedding reception on the beach at Malibu, complete with shoeless guests and celebrants. Photos: John Barber.*

🍃 (Left) Under the cover of a massive tent, supports wrapped in greenery suited this garden theme perfectly. Photo: Harold Hechler Associates, Ltd.

🍃 (Above) Fresh fruits and vegetables tumble onto a deliciously appealing buffet table. Photo: G. Gregory Geiger.

🍃 (Inset) As pretty as they are tasty, hors d'oeuvres share space with flowers on a silver tray. Photo: Thomas Preti Caterers.

Bridal Style

The art of presentation as mastered by talented ice craftsmen.

❧ (This page) Leafy bunches of grapes and fresh, colorful flowers compose a three-dimensional design when suspended in these frozen bowls.

❧ (Opposite) An underwater reef was recreated to hold an icy cold display of seafood. Photos for this spread: Iceculture Inc.

❧ (Opposite) Nestled in lush surroundings, these guests enjoyed the weather at a secluded garden reception. Photo: Georgia Sheron.

❧ (Top, left) The bride's and groom's chairs at this sunny reception are wrapped in tulle and flowers. Photo: Ortiz Photography.

❧ (Bottom, left) This classical quartet played in the shelter of shady trees. Photo: Joseph C. Pecoraro.

❧ (Below) The sounds of a drum and bagpipes drifted through the air at this reception site. Photo: Richard Fanning.

Here and there, tables overflow with gifts and food.
❧ *(Above)* A basket brimming with bread and flowers serves as the centerpiece on this buffet table. *Photo: P. Melville for Culinary Architect Catering.*
❧ *(Left)* Ceremony scrolls held by gold bands are displayed on a silver tray. *Photo: Georgia Sheron.*

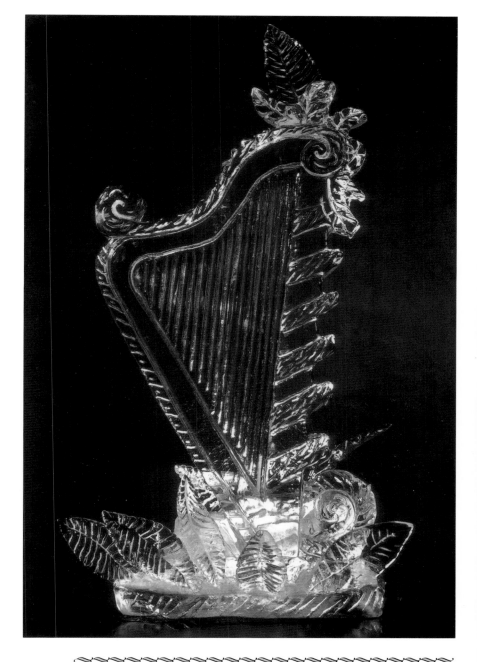

Elaborate ice sculptures are often requested to accompany seafood stations or raw bars which require constant chilling.

🦐 (Above) Artistry in ice: This graceful harp was worked in painstaking detail by Scott Rella of Ice Sculpture Designs. Photo: Rob Rich.

🦐 (Right) At this reception, an icy windmill marks the spot where seafood is served. Photo: G. Gregory Geiger.

Hotels, restaurants, and clubs have skilled professionals who can arrange any kind of reception, down to the smallest details.

❧ (Above) A luxurious hotel setting was made even richer with the addition of wedding flowers and formal table settings. Photo: Harold Hechler Associates, Ltd.

❧ (Left) Ribbon-tied flowers adorn a service tray: one of the small touches that add so much. Photo: Georgia Sheron.

❧ (Opposite) At The Rainbow Room, one of New York City's most sophisticated restaurants, a bride and groom pose amid the glamour. Photo: Harold Hechler Associates, Ltd.

🦋 After a day of dignified rituals and exchanging serious vows, it's time to cut loose. This bride and groom are ready for a casual group photo surrounded by their wedding party and a circle of friends. Photo: Jonathan Farrer.

The cutting of the cake is a sweet tradition.

(Below) Couples sometimes miss their marks—and this bride loved every moment. Photo: Michael Kohl.

(Top left) The same bride's parents share a bit of cake at their 1960 wedding. Photo: Dan Waggoner.

(Bottom, left) It's the perfect photo opportunity—and, yes, forks are still used on occasion. Photo: Maureen DeFries for Laurie Klein Gallery.

All good things must end, and leaving the reception is often done with a flourish.

🐁 *(Above)* This horse-drawn carriage, bedecked with flowers and bows, waits to carry the happy couple away after an at-home reception. Photo: Brown and Barton.

🐁 *(Top, left)* Off to their honeymoon, these newlyweds depart in a shower of rose petals. Photo: Richard Fanning.

🐁 *(Bottom, left)* Confetti is also a festive choice for a couple's send-off. Photo: Georgia Sheron.

🐁 *(Opposite)* A bride and groom wave farewell to their guests from the rumble seat of a vintage automobile. Photo: Maureen DeFries for Laurie Klein Gallery.

THE
CAKE

he tradition of the wedding cake began in ancient Rome. As an offering to Jupiter, the groom tasted the barley or wheat cake, then broke it over the head of the bride; guests shared the fallen crumbs. In the Middle Ages, newlyweds kissed over a stack of sweetened buns. When a French pastry chef iced one such stack, the modern wedding cake was born.

(Preceding spread) Meticulous workmanship is evident in every flower and streamer on this wedding cake by talented baker Kevin Pavlina. Photo: Focal Point Studio.

(Left) Pink roses cascade along the tiers of this traditional cake. Photo: Joseph C. Pecoraro.

(Opposite) A sweet cherub tops this exquisite domed cake reminiscent of fine Wedgwood china. Cake by Cheryl Kleinman; concept: Donna Ferrari, Bride's magazine.

*A*lthough this confection has gone through many transformations along the way, the ritual of cutting the cake is still an important one, steeped in meaning. Sharing a champagne toast and the tradition of watching the bride and groom feed each other a sweet sample of cake are highlights of any wedding celebration. Therefore, the baker you choose must understand the vision you have of this special cake.

*W*hen you interview bakers, ask a series of questions. For instance, can the baker reproduce the style of a cake you spotted in a book or magazine—but in very different flavors? If you choose a design from a personal portfolio, will the baker alter an aspect of the decoration or recipe for you? Is the baker experienced at creating custom-designed cakes or unique shapes? Are only natural ingredients used? How soon before your celebration will the cake be baked? Finally, take a taste test: once you've come close to a decision, ask to try a smaller sample cake before making your final choice.

∼ CAKE DESIGNS ∼

*T*oday's wedding cakes come from the kitchens of some very talented bakers and are triumphs of both design and taste. They may display artful details or whimsical touches, petals made of frosting and shaped into perfect flowers, and sweet cake layers filled with fresh cremes or fruit. Some cakes are circled with designs as delicate as those on a bridal gown. Others are trimmed in motifs that echo the reception's decor. In any design, a cake is a treasured memory for the bride and groom.

*C*akes have become increasingly important elements in today's more opulent weddings. Bakers now set out to make edible works of art to please more sophisticated tastes.

Once you have determined the style of your wedding cake, discuss with your baker the many decorations, fillings, and flavors that he or she is able to create.

No longer content with the usual recipes, newlyweds want cakes that make a statement—inside and out. Spicy carrot, tangy lemon creme, and mocha mousse are among the many options offered by expressive bakers.

Ellen Baumwoll, an award-winning baker and owner of Bijoux Doux ("Sweet Jewels") Specialty Cakes in New York City, notes that "the majority of couples I work with choose chocolate cake or a rich chocolate truffle filling.

(Left) White chocolate "ribbons" and roses, adorn this delicate wedding cake. Photo: Stephane Colbert.

(Opposite) Sweet ambrosia best describes the sight of a treasure-laden table and the heavenly aroma of the wedding cake. This one, by Sylvia Weinstock, is lavished with handmade lilies of the valley and other sugar-dough blooms. Photo: Bill Margerin.

Another popular request is for a hazelnut/almond cake I often make for weddings—but with a chocolate filling!"

The way to please a wide variety of tastes is by asking that each tier be a different flavor—then there's sure to be something for everyone.

To complement the luscious inside, nothing less than pulled sugar ribbons, gold icing, or an intricate cake top will do to adorn the outside of your cake. Surface decoration can take on many looks: piping, lettering, ribbons, chocolate curls, trelliswork, and hand-rolled roses can create an individualized look. And sugar can be shaped into the most marvelous things: lacy edges, tiny marzipan fruits, a garden of flowers.

Cile Bellefleur-Burbidge, widely recognized as a leader in the art of cake decorating, captures a Victorian style in her creations that are a marvel to behold. From her home's kitchen in Danvers, Massachusetts, she turns out towering cakes that are covered with her signature touches. "I use many scrolls, fences, floral arrangements, and latticework as decoration. Everything is created by piping royal icing onto a buttercream frosting. And

edible gold leaf is now a popular accent that I've also used many times."

For a very different look, a rolled fondant icing is the preferred topping for many bakers because its smooth finish is easy to decorate or quilt with the proper tools. For baker Baumwoll, fondant is actually a necessity when she's working one of her favorite styles of confections. "I design an Americanized version of the Australian cake, which is characterized by a smooth surface with beveled edges and lots of fine decorations. The intricate lace and embroidery work is done with an extremely tiny tube—the results actually resemble fabric. Fondant, or similar icings, such as rolled white chocolate or marzipan, must be used to create the effect."

For many bakers, the wedding itself is the richest source of decorating ideas. Cheryl Kleinman, who operates Cheryl Kleinman Cakes in New York City, feels that the cake should somehow reflect the wedding's theme or the bride and groom's personalities. "I like to have the cake echo elements of the wedding. The theme or color scheme should somehow be matched in feeling by the couple's cake. It's a very personal point, and I work with them to create exactly what they envision, since everyone has quite different ideas. In fact, the only thing many of my clients now commonly request is that their cakes have a strong, bold design that can be seen from across the room, because so many of them are on display throughout the reception."

(Left) An exceptionally skilled hand fashioned this marvelous cake, which features sugary roses and lilies of the valley. Photo: Jan Douglas Armor Photography.
(Opposite) Perfect rows of pink and white latticework cover this intricate gazebo cake by Cile Bellefleur-Burbidge. An urn of pink flowers is sheltered under the canopy. Photo: Douglas Christian.

~ CAKE TOPS ~

A miniature marvel, the top of your cake will have a big impact on the overall finished look, so choose a style that sweetly complements the cake's overall design. Flowers, both fresh-cut and sugar dough, are beautiful additions. Traditional tops, such as a bride and groom, are still making appearances on towering treats, but today most wedding cakes are designed without them.

*M*any of today's bakers bring an artistic background to their work and can design spectacular tops. Bellefleur-Burbidge has seen a rise in the request for miniature gazebos. Kleinman sculpted a Hawaiian island, complete with a couple atop a volcano. Baumwoll created a replica of the Sacred Heart Church in Prague for one architect-groom who greatly admired that building. She also once shaped an airplane from sugar paste for a couple who met in flight. And the Roman Colosseum was requested by another groom whose fiancée was of Italian heritage. (*He* provided a small pair of lions, one wearing a wedding veil, the other wearing a tie!)

*F*or couples who want a wedding cake to reflect their personalities, bakers can accommodate almost any request. The right tools and a practiced hand can turn any idea into reality.

A unique cake top also serves as a keepsake, since many newlyweds still follow the tradition of freezing the top layer of their cake and eating it on their first wedding anniversary. Those who have carefully preserved the confection can enjoy an evening—and a dessert—filled with sweet memories.

~ THE CAKE TABLE ~

*T*he wedding reception culminates in the cutting of a fabulous cake, designed just for you for this day. Anything that treats your senses of smell, sight, and taste to such a wonderful lift deserves a showcase of its own. Thus, once you have commissioned your ideal wedding cake, plan to display it on a suitably designed cake table. Many couples choose to have the cake on display throughout the reception, others have the table rolled into the room after the meal, signaling the end of the festivities. Either way, this detail requires special attention.

*K*eeping in mind that your cake is the centerpiece, concentrate on adding elements that enhance its design. Display an elegant cake knife and server set in cut crystal or sterling silver and tied with rich ribbons; a beautiful tablecloth; the bride's bouquet; and perhaps a grouping of slender champagne flutes.

～ THE GROOM'S CAKE ～

*B*efore the introduction of powdery white flour and leavening in eighteenth-century America, the wedding cake was traditionally a dense, rich fruitcake. Today, the "groom's cake" carries on this custom, although chocolate has replaced fruit in popularity.

Generally just one layer, this confection is often baked in a shape or topped with a design that depicts the groom's interests or hobbies. The cake is cut and served at the reception or distributed in individual boxes to departing guests. A single woman who places a sliver of the cake under her pillow that night will supposedly dream of her future husband.

～ CHAMPAGNE AND TOASTS ～

When Dom Perignon, a seventeenth-century Benedictine monk in France, invented champagne, he called it a "drink for lovers." Today, champagne, the most festive and glamorous of all wines, is the preferred beverage for toasting at wedding celebrations.

Champagnes run from very dry to sweet. *Natural* or *Brut* are the driest. *Sec* is a little sweeter, and *Demi-Sec* is even sweeter. For wedding cakes, a Sec or Demi-sec champagne is often recommended.

One legend has it that toasting began in ancient Greece when a host drank before his guests to prove his wine was not poisoned. Revelers in France would pass around wine and toasted bread. When the toastee received the glass, he emptied it and ate the bread.

At a wedding reception, once the guests' flutes have been filled, the first person to raise a glass in a toast is usually the best man. The groom then offers toasts to the bride, his parents, and hers. The bride might also choose to join the toasting, followed by family, members of the wedding party, and guests who wish to add their tributes.

Here are samples of some traditional toasts:

Grow old along with me!
The best is yet to be,
The last of life, for which the first was made.
—ROBERT BROWNING

Here's to the happy man: All the world loves a lover.
—RALPH WALDO EMERSON

Look down you gods,
And on this couple drop a blessed crown.
—SHAKESPEARE

May you grow old on one pillow.
—ARMENIAN SAYING

❧ (Opposite) A trail of apricot-colored orchids, hand sculpted of sugar dough in exacting detail, graces this dotted Swiss cake by James E. Kennedy. Photo: John W. Corbett.

❧ (Left) Bundles of white flowers and green leaves tumble down around a cake of graduated tiers by Sylvia Weinstock. Photo: Stephane Colbert.

❧ (Below) Iced in gold and draped in white "fabric," this creation by Cheryl Kleinman is totally edible. Photo: Carol Seitz.

🐝 (Opposite) This
magnificent confection
was designed on paper
by the client, then exe-
cuted by the baker,
Albert Kumin. Royal
icing lacework and
elaborate scrolls blan-
ket the tiers; miniature
marzipan fruits, white-
chocolate angels, and
the pulled sugar basket
topper are astounding
in their detail. Photo:
Bill Margerin.

🐝 (Right) This med-
ley of colorful
flowers looks like the
bride's bouquet, but is
actually her wedding
cake. Designed by
Sylvia Weinstock,
these posies rest on a
golden cake base.
Photo: Stephane Colbert.

🍫 *(Above) Chocolate lovers can have the wedding cake of their dreams, such as this ribbon-tied confection by Ellen Baumwoll of Bijoux Doux Specialty Cakes. Photo: Fred Marcus.*

❧ (Above, left) Patti Paige was inspired by Art Deco when she created this tiered cake covered in a black, white, and gold design. Photo: Vincent B. Lee.

❧ (Above, right) Softly rounded tiers are studded in a pearly dotted Swiss pattern, styled after the ethereal fabric of the same name. Peachy marzipan roses circle the tiers. From "The Cake Bible," by Rose Levy Beranbaum. Photo: Vincent B. Lee.

❧ (Right) Chocolate ribbons and roses top each tier of this delectable cake by Cheryl Kleinman. Such rich, dark confections might also serve as a groom's cakes. Photo: Tony Cenicola.

(Clockwise from below, right) Only a practiced hand can create the extraordinary details such as those on this cake by James E. Kennedy. This single layer is crowned with swirls, hearts, and other intricate motifs. Photo: John W. Corbett; all white and piped with a pattern of Grecian swathes, this tiered cake is topped with fresh flowers. Photo: G. Gregory Geiger; a frilly skirt flares around the base of this elegant cake by James E. Kennedy. Photo: John W. Corbett; lilies of the valley were recreated in icing for this cake with a fresh-flower topper. Photo: Phyllis L. Keenan.

(Opposite) The artful eye and steady skills of Kevin Pavlina are evident in the amazing structure of this wedding cake. Photo: Lisa Charles.

❧ *(Above) From James E. Kennedy, a single square layer festooned with lacework and a sugary gardenia may be
fitting for a bridal shower or a small reception. Photo: John W. Corbett.*

❧ *(Opposite, clockwise from top) Ribbons and flowers dress two squared tiers with lacy edges by Ellen Baumwoll of
Bijoux Doux Specialty Cakes. Photo: JoVon; a lattice cage of royal icing surrounds an octagonal cake with rose
detailing; dainty sprigs of lily of the valley were piped all around this pretty little cake that's also suitable for a bridal
shower or engagement party. A real lily of the valley, wrapped in a lace hankie, is the topper. Both cakes from
"The Cake Bible" by Rose Levy Beranbaum. Photos: Vincent B. Lee.*

~~~~~~

🍃 *(Above) Handmade flowers are scattered atop one tier iced in rolled fondant; from Cheryl Kleinman Cakes. Photo: Tony Cenicola.*

🍃 *(Opposite, clockwise from near right) A baked basket of flowers—a wonderfully appealing sight on the cake table. Photo/cake: Alexandra Troy for Culinary Architect Catering; dome tiers are decorated with a rope of brilliantly colored sugar dough flowers, by Ellen Baumwoll of Bijoux Doux Specialty Cakes. Photo: Judy Smith; the delicate light from votive candles reveals the fine dotted Swiss and lace details that cover this tiered cake. Photo: Jan Douglas Armor Photography.*

~~~~~~

🍃 (Opposite) A Japanese couple in traditional dress cut into a regally designed cake topped with white swans. Photo: Magnum Photo.

🍃 (Center) Especially ideal for weddings during the holiday season, this cake by Colette Peters is ringed in fruity garlands and wreaths and edged with gold braids and bows. Photo: Bernard Vidal.

🍃 (Above) Gold dragées and ribbons swirl around a cake blanketed in buttercream and bedecked with fresh flowers. From "The Cake Bible" by Rose Levy Beranbaum. Photo: Vincent B. Lee.

Three masterful examples of the baker's art, by Cile Bellefleur-Burbidge.

❧ (Opposite) Pink and white perfection: draped latticework is crowned with an urn of handmade flowers.

❧ (Above, left) Edible architecture, down to the soft flowers and majestic dome.

❧ (Above, right) Tiny violets, shaped by a skilled hand, mix in with other delicately crafted flowers on these lattice-covered tiers. All photos: Douglas Christian.

❧ (Right) This reception ended with a sweet display of petit fours and miniature wedding cakes. Photo: Georgia Sheron.

❧ *(Below)* Shades of white provide subtle contrast on this piped dome confection from Cheryl Kleinman Cakes. *Photo: Tony Cenicola.*

❧ *(Top right)* Miniature grape clusters are tucked among the intricate iced details on this tiered creation by Ellen Baumwoll of Bijoux Doux Specialty Cakes. *Photo: Valeche Studio/R. Nazario.*

❧ *(Bottom right)* A wispy spun sugar base circles a tiered cheesecake trimmed with gold lamé ribbons and wild violets. From "The Cake Bible" by Rose Levy Beranbaum. *Photo: Vincent B. Lee.*

❧ *(Opposite)* Nestled in a cloud of tulle, a tiered cake tower is dramatically flanked by smaller cakes that are covered in pastel sugar flowers. *Cakes: Kevin Pavlina. Photo: Focal Point Studio.*

~ BRIDAL STYLE SOURCE GUIDE ~

Source
Guide

Wedding Photographers

JAN DOUGLAS ARMOR
Armor Photography
2701 East Main Road
Portsmouth, RI 02871

JON BARBER
Barber Photography
34071 LaPlaza
Suite 100
Dana Point, CA 92629

BROWN AND BARTON
S. Ribaut Road
Beaufort, SC 29902
Dana Point, CA 92629

STEPHANE COLBERT
Walnut Tree Road
Sandy Hook, CT 06482

JOHN W. CORBETT
928 West Main Road
Middletown, RI 02840

MAUREEN EDWARDS DE FRIES
518 Federal Road
Brookfield, CT 06804

ELLIS-TAYLOR PHOTOGRAPHERS
20265 Ventura Blvd.
Woodland Hills, CA 91364

ROBBI ERNST
June Wedding Inc.
1331 Burnham Avenue
Las Vegas, NV 89104

RICHARD FANNING
Richard Fanning Photography
Whitney Street
Westport, CT 06880

JONATHAN FARRER
Jonathan Farrer Photo Inc.
5001 Odessa Ave.
Encino, CA 91436

G. GREGORY GEIGER
Wheeler's Farms Road
Orange, CT 06477

MARIPAT GOODWIN PHOTOGRAPHER
57 Old Highway
Southbury, CT 06488

DAVID HECHLER
Harold Hechler Associates, Ltd.
67 Gladstone Road
New Rochelle, NY 19804

PHYLLIS KEENAN PHOTOGRAPHY
9 Williams Road
Danbury, CT 06810

LAURIE KLEIN
Laurie Klein Gallery
290 Federal Road
Brookfield, CT 06804

MICHAEL KOHL
Kohl Photography and Video
906 Monroe Street
Santa Clara, CA 95050

LEONARD LEWIS
328 Central Park West
New York, NY 10025

CHARLOTTE MAHER
Maher Photography
47 Anderson Rd
Sherman, CT 06784

JEFF MEYERS
Wine Country Wedding
Photography
683 Draco Drive
Petaluma, CA 94954

NANCY MULLER
Rocky Mountain Images
PO Box 1813
Vail, CO 81658

CHRISTINE NEWMAN
Persona Grata Photography
107 Sixth Street
Hoboken, NJ 07030

ORTIZ PHOTOGRAPHY
18207 Mc Durmott
East Irvine, CA 92714

JOSEPH PECORARO
Joseph's Photography
189 Middlesex Ave.
Chester, CT 06412

GEORGIA SHERON
Georgia Sheron Photography
228 Main Street
Oakville, CT 06779

BILL STOCKWELL
Photography by Bill Stockwell
2 Garden Ave.
San Rafael, CA 94903

FRIDRICK TIEDEMANN
Fridrick Tiedemann Photography
906 E. Belleview Circle
Beaufort, SC 29902

DANIEL WAGGONER
Danick Studio, Inc.
17710 Chatsworth Street
Grenada Hills, CA 91344

Commercial Photographers

CYNTHIA BROWN
448 West 37th Street
New York, NY 10018

TONY CENICOLA
325 West 37th Street
New York, NY 10018

DOUGLAS CHRISTIAN
443 Albany Street
Boston, MA 02118

FOCAL POINT STUDIO
3343 Grand River
Farmington, MI 48335-3521

MARILI FORASTIERI
426 W. Broadway
New York, NY 10011

ANDREW FRENCH
698 West End Ave.
New York, NY 10025

~ 239 ~

TIM GEANY
Contact: Yellen Lashapelle,
212-838-3170

SCOTT HAGENDORF
527 Hudson Street
New York, NY 10014

GEORGE HOLZ
Contact: Elka Kristo-Nagy,
212-505-5607

IRAIDA ICAZA
50 White Street
New York, NY 10013

DAN LECCA
35-36 85th Street
Jackson Heights, NY 11372

VINCENT LEE
155 Wooster Street
New York, NY 10012

CRAIG MERRILL
259 Church Street
San Fransisco, CA 94114

EMILY MILLER
124 Thompson Street
New York, NY 10012

GEORGE OTERO
330 East 46th Street
New York, NY 10017

PHOTOGRAFY MAHDAVIAN
Canal Street Station,
PO Box 1850
New York, NY 10013

ROB RICH
112 12th Ave.
Sea Cliff, NJ 11579

JEREMY SAMUELSON
1188 S. LaBrea
Los Angeles, CA 90019

CAROL SEITZ
61 Duncan Ave.
Jersey City, NJ 07304

BICO STUPAKOFF
Contact: Clare Keeble,
212-255-3252

THE STUDIO
296 Brick Blvd.
Brick, NJ

ANTOINE VERGLAS
Contact: Jean Gabriel Kauss,
212-779-4440

BERNARD VIDAL
Contact: Alice Morales
212-255-3252

Caterers

CULINARY ARCHITECTS INC.
475 Port Washington Blvd.
Port Washington, NY 11050

GLORIOUS FOOD
522 East 74th Street
New York, NY 10021

MOVABLE FEAST
284 Prospect Park West
Brooklyn, NY 11215

THOMAS PRETI CATERERS
22-10 42nd Street
Astoria, NY 11105

Ice Sculptures

ICECULTURE INC.
PO Box 232
Hensall, Ontario Canada

ICE SCULPTURE DESIGN
697 Acorn Street #D
Deer Park, NY 11729

Accessories

CAROLINA AMATO ACCESSORIES
15 West 37th Street
New York, NY 10016

CHICAGO BEAD WORKS
1998 Imio Street
Lisle, IL 60532

PETER FOX SHOES
105 Thompson Street
New York, NY 10012

712 Montana Ave.
Santa Monica, CA 90403

STUART WIETZMAN & CO. (Shoes)
625 Madison Ave.
New York, NY 10019

T & G BRIDAL VEILS
131 West 35th Street
New York, NY 10018

Wedding Cakes

ELLEN BAUMWOLL
Bijoux Doux Specialty Cakes and
Pastries
304 Mulberry Street
New York, NY 10012

CILE BELLFLEUR-BURBIDGE
12 Stafford Road
Danvers, MA

JAMES E. KENNEDY
231 New Boston Road
Fall River, MA

CHERYL KLEINMAN
448 Atlantic Ave.
Broooklyn NY 11217

KEVIN PAVLINA
PO Box 246
Northville, MI 48167

COLETTE PETERS
327 W. 11th Street
New York, NY 10014

SYLVIA WEINSTOCK
273 Church Street
New York, NY 10014

Wedding Dresses

AMSALE
347 W. 39th Street
New York, NY 10018

CAROLINA HERRERA, LTD.
501 Seventh Ave.
New York, NY

CHANEL
5 East 57th Street
New York, NY 10022

CHRISTIAN DIOR
791 Park of Commerce Blvd.
Boca Raton, FL 33487

DOLCE & GABBANA
532 Broadway
New York, NY 10012

JESSICA MCCLINTOCK
1412 Broadway
New York, NY 10018

JIM HJELM INTERNATIONAL LTD.
501 Seventh Ave.
New York, NY 10018

LAURA ASHLEY INC.
714 Madison Ave.
New York, NY

LILI
1117 East Main Street
Alhambra, CA 91801

MICHELE PICCIONE FOR
ALFRED ANGELO
791 Park of Commerce Blvd.
Boca Raton, FL 33487

PRISCILLA OF BOSTON
40 Cambridge St.
Charlestown, MA 02129

ULLA-MAIJA
24 West 40th Street
New York, NY 10018

VAN LEAR BRIDALS, INC.
1375 Broadway
New York, NY

VERA WANG BRIDAL
COLLECTION
225 West 39th Street
New York, NY 10018

CASTLE & PIERPONT
401 East 76th Street
New York, NY 10021

CREATIVE FLORALS
1005 N. Salisbury Blvd.
Salisbury, MD 21801

ELAN FLOWERS
148 Duane Street
New York, NY 10013

DIANE JAMISON
Personal Flowers
4 South Pinehurst Ave.
New York, NY 10033

VENA LEFFERTS
1024 Olive Street
Santa Barbara, CA 93101-1409

OPPIZZI & COMPANY
818 Greenwich Ave.
New York, NY 10014

ANDREW PASCOE
471 West Main
Oyster Bay, NY 11771

REINCARNATION
(freeze-dried flowers)
5377 Hiatus Road
Sunset, FL 33351

RENNY
505 Park Avenue
New York, NY 10022

ELIZABETH RYAN FLORAL DESIGN
411 East 9th Street
New York, NY 10009

Reception Sites

AIR PIRATE BALLOON ACADEMY
New Jersey 1-800-4Hot-Air

BEANO'S CABIN
Beaver Creek, CO

DISNEY WORLD AND
DISNEYLAND FANTASY
WEDDINGS
Orlando, FL
and Los Angeles, CA

HAMMERSMITH FARM
Ocean Drive
Newport, RI 02840

KNOTT'S BERRY FARM
8039 Beach Boulevard
Buena Park, CA 90620

THE PHILADELPHIA ZOO
34th and Girard Ave.
Philadelphia, PA 19104

UNIVERSAL STUDIOS
100 Universal City Plaza
Universal City, CA 91608

Lighting

BENTLEY MEEKER STAGING AND
LIGHTING
426 E. 91 st Street
New York, NY 10128

Florists

ABOUT FLOWERS
79 Main Street
South Meriden, CT 06450

PAUL BOTT BEAUTIFUL FLOWERS
1305 Madison Ave.
New York, NY

CHARLES R. CASE
The Flower Basket
995 Post Road East
Westport, CT 06880

Wedding Consultants

A WEDDING MADE IN PARADISE
PO Box 986
Kihei, Maui Hawaii 96753
1-800-453-3440

FANTASIA
St. Thomas, US Virgin Islands
1-800-FANTASA

WINE COUNTRY WEDDINGS
6795 Washington Street
Yountville, CA 94599-1353

Invitations

CALLIGRAPHERS' INK
944 Danbury Road
Georgetown, CT 06829

FAERIE TALE DESIGNS
Michele T. Juliard
542 Main St. Southbury, CT 06488

~ INDEX ~